FREEDOM FROM FEAR

First published 1990
The Institute of Irish Studies
The Queen's University of Belfast
University Road, Belfast

ISBN 0 85389 371 3

Typeset by Textflow Services Ltd
Printed by W. & G. Baird Ltd, Antrim

FREEDOM FROM FEAR

Churches Together
in Northern Ireland

edited by

Simon Lee

The proceedings of a conference organised by the Churches' Central Committee for Community Work and held at Loughry College, Cookstown, on 27 September 1990.

CONTENTS

Page

FOREWORD

We urge all men and women of goodwill to read this book and pray that they might find inspiration from the efforts of others in the Gospel work of reconciliation. We are glad that the Churches' Central Committee for Community Work, created by our four churches, brought Christians together for the conference which is recorded in these pages. We also rejoice in the fact that the positive side of the churches' contribution has been highlighted. We hope and pray that Christians throughout this part of the world will answer the call to action which has come from Cookstown.

The Most Rev Robert Eames   Church of Ireland
The Rev William Buchanan   Methodist
The Right Rev Finlay Holmes   Presbyterian
The Most Rev Cahal Daly   Roman Catholic

PART I

INTRODUCTION

EDITORIAL PREFACE

This book is based on an inter-church conference. The 175 people who attended and the Churches' Central Committee for Community Work (CCCCW), who organised the meeting, felt that the proceedings ought to be more widely available. The CCCCW asked me if I would edit the book. I would in turn ask two favours of those who read what follows. First, after reflecting on the work of the groups who presented reports to the conference, would you please consider whether you can help to promote this kind of work? The way forward rests on little local initiatives, which are within your power, if you live in Northern Ireland. If you live elsewhere, there are many ways in which you can support the work of local people. Second, would you please let the Churches' Central Committee for Community Work know what you are doing? They would love to help you, if you so wish and if they can assist. They would also like to be able to pool experiences so that when groups from another part of Northern Ireland seek advice, they can refer them to you. At the conference on which this book is based, for example, leaders of Protestant and Catholic youth clubs, both of whom were looking for a partner club outside their immediate areas, found each other. Time and again, somebody suggested an initiative, to be told that it had happened elsewhere - that these were the problems, these the possible solutions. There is so much Good News which needs to be shared.

The swift publication of this book has depended on many people doing many favours. In particular, I would like to thank the CCCCW, especially their development officer Tom O'Connor and their Chairman Rev Tom Craig, for having the vision and enthusiasm to call the conference. Their secretary, Mrs Wilma Beatty, has worked heroically to produce transcripts of the discussions. Jenny Greenaway, Karen Agnew and Nancy Bowman of Queen's then produced the typescript of this book, with their customary speed, efficiency and good humour. Project Planning organised the detail of the conference. The Central Community Relations Unit (CCRU) has generously funded publication. Tony McCusker of the CCRU deserves special thanks and praise. Dr Brian Walker and the Institute of Irish Studies have been supremely efficient and swift in publishing the book. Above all, the local groups who told their stories at the conference deserve our thanks and admiration. The best way in which we can thank all these people is by following where they have led.

SIMON LEE
Professor of Jurisprudence
The Queen's University
Belfast

All Saints' Day, 1990

CHAIRMAN'S INTRODUCTION

Rev Tom Craig

I would like to welcome you all to the conference and thank all those who helped inspire or organise the conference, particularly those at the CCCCW, the CCRU and Project Planning, who in their various ways are responsible for the day.

The Apostle Paul wrote to the Church at Ephesus; 'I urge you, then - I who am in prison because I serve the Lord: live a life that measures up to the standard God set when he called you. Be always humble, gentle and patient. Show you love by being tolerant with one another. Do your best to preserve the unity which the Spirit gives by means of the peace that binds you together. There is one body and one Spirit, just as there is one hope to which God has called you. There is one Lord, one faith, one baptism; there is one God and Father of all mankind, who is Lord of all, works through all, and is in all.

... by speaking the truth in a spirit of love, we must grow up in every way to Christ, who is the head. Under His control all the different parts of the body fit together by every joint with which it is provided. So when each separate part works as it should, the whole body grows and builds itself up through love'. (Ephesians chapter 4 verses 1-6 and 15-16, read from Today's English Version, The Good News Bible).

Let us stand and pray.

O God the Eternal Father of us all, we thank you
for the opportunities of this day
for bringing us to this Conference
for the love of friends and family
for the assurance of your eternal and unchanging love
made known to us through Jesus Christ.

O Lord, lead us today in whatever we do,
and help us always by the gift of your grace.

We begin our day with you.
May we continue in your presence, and
at the end of the day
may we rest in the confidence that you are still with us.

We ask for your blessing upon our Conference.
Be merciful to the weakness of our best endeavours.
If there has been, if there is, anything unworthy in our
   motives, forgive.
if we have been blind to the obvious and the necessary,
if there is anything lacking in our preparations,
through your Spirit
compensate for what we lack.
Inflame us with a care for the good name of Jesus.
Build us up in true religion.
Feed us with what is true, noble and worthy,
with what everyone must acknowledge to be good.

Hear us now as we pray as Jesus taught us, saying:

Our Father, who art in Heaven, hallowed by Thy Name.
Thy Kingdom come,
Thy will be done on earth as it is in Heaven.
Give us this day our daily bread.
And forgive us our debts as we forgive our debtors.
And lead us not into temptation, but deliver us from evil.
For Thine is the Kingdom, and the Power and the Glory for ever.

Amen

Our keynote address is to be given by Simon Lee. His three young
children, his wife and he came to Northern Ireland two years ago
when he was appointed to the Chair of Jurisprudence at The
Queen's University of Belfast. He comes to us with a sense of
perspective, having lived, studied and worked around the world.
Although his academic discipline is the philosophy of law, he has an
abiding interest in religious matters. His first book, *Law & Morals*,
(Oxford University Press, 1986) discussed such issues as the role of
the churches in public debate about the law on embryo experi-
ments. His last book, *Believing Bishops* (with Peter Stanford, Faber,
1990) analysed the need for prophetic leadership in the Catholic

and Anglican churches. His next book, *The Cost of Free Speech* (Faber, November 1990) builds on his work for InterFaith on the Muslim reaction to the Rushdie affair, as well as reflecting on events closer to home, such as the government's restrictions on the broadcasting of those who support violence. He has explored the problems of Northern Ireland in his play, *Day of Judgment,* first performed at Queen's earlier this year. Professor Lee also writes for newspapers and appears on radio and television in England and Northern Ireland. In particular, he is a regular contributor to the religious weekly, the *Catholic Herald.*

PART II

KEYNOTE ADDRESS

FREEDOM FROM FEAR & THE CHURCHES IN NORTHERN IRELAND

by

Simon Lee

Fear is the churches' greatest problem in Northern Ireland. Freedom from fear can be the churches' greatest contribution to our lives here. I am not primarily talking about fear of the men of violence. The churches in Northern Ireland sometimes give the impression of being more worried by women of intelligence, or lay people of independence, than they are by men of violence. Fear of each other's dogmas, power, intentions, aspirations, all these fears bedevil the churches (and you can take 'bedevil' as literally as you like). So, freedom from fear is my theme. Let me now signpost four ways in which I hope to develop that theme.

First, it is quite wrong to talk in terms of the churches here failing us, or of us failing the churches. The churches ARE us. You may have heard of the international toy retailers, TOYS 'R' US. Well, CHURCHES 'R' US would be a good slogan for the work of the organisers of this conference. So let me re-phrase my opening comments. Fear is *our* greatest problem, freedom from fear is the way forward for *us*, freedom from the fear of violent men, articulate women, fear of the unknown, fear of the other.

Second, who other than Christ has been an effective preacher of this message, of freedom from fear? My own hero in this regard would be Martin Luther King. Although it will come as a shock to those in this part of the world who think that Martin Luther King's mission in life was to inspire Northern Ireland's local, largely Catholic, civil rights movement in the late sixties, Martin Luther King was, of course, a Protestant. Who put the Luther in Martin Luther King? He was a Baptist Minister whose public or political life in search of justice was wonderfully inspired by the gospels, by a similar religious faith to that professed by many inhabitants of this narrow ground. The base from which he organised the freedom marches was the Southern Christian Leadership Conference. He clearly saw himself as a preacher, definitely not a priest.

Third, if alongside Martin Luther King's message, we had to point to one other Christian to exemplify the way forward for our churches, then I would nominate Mother Teresa. By which I mean that the best hope for the future of our churches here is if we listen to, watch, and follow, the example of the holy women of all denominations and faiths, in all parts of the world, who live a simple life of prayer and love.

Fourth, if you remember those Bob Hope and Bing Crosby films, The Road to ..., ask yourself what title you would choose for a film about Northern Ireland. I would choose the road, not to Cookstown, nor to Dublin, London, Belfast, nor even to Brussels, but the roads to *Jericho* and *Emmaus*. I mean by referring to the Road to Emmaus, for example, that just like those two disciples running away from Jerusalem after the Crucifixion, we walk with Christ, yet do not recognise Him as our companion. We are too scared by current events to notice Christ among us. But then, we learn of the disciples on the road to Emmaus, that 'their eyes were opened and they recognised Him'.

Putting those four points together, the message which Northern Ireland needs from our churches, from US, is the message proclaimed by Christ and His true followers, like Martin Luther King *and* Mother Teresa, black *and* white, male *and* female, Protestant *and* Catholic, on all the roads which lead to Emmaus or Jericho and back to Jerusalem. The message is that the most precious freedom is FREEDOM FROM FEAR. We are all too afraid, afraid of paramilitaries, of militarymilitaries, of what others will think, of losing power, of gaining power, afraid of the unknown, afraid of 'them'. You, in your brave steps to co-operate with one another, are facing that fear, armed only with your faith in Christ.

In this conference, I hope we can learn how to translate that message into practical help for all Northern Irish pilgrims on the road to Emmaus. You will shortly tell us about your work together. In this address, I aim to show how reflection on our Christian faith can complement, and enable or empower, your practical work.

But why me? Why have I been asked to speak to you today? After all, you will have gathered two things about me: my accent sounds suspiciously English and my job sounds suspiciously legal, and academic as well. The perspective, then, is that of an outsider who has only been living here for two years. But as Henry James once

wrote, there are aspects of even very large mountains which cannot
be appreciated by those who live on them but which can be
glimpsed by a single glance from afar. It is no bad thing to have
commentators who can bring a sense of perspective.

There is now in London an exhibition of Monet's great series
paintings, including many of the studies he made of the cathedral
at Rouen. Each picture captures the cathedral in a different light.
I have found it helpful in many contexts to think of observations
as offering only 'one view of the cathedral'. Although Monet
painted from only one position, we could imagine people painting
from all around the cathedral. Each painter tells us something
about the cathedral, but also something about themselves and their
vantage-point. Some view events here from the west, some from the
east, some from the left, others from the right, some see only
darkness, others light. No single picture is right or wrong. In order
to deepen our understanding of the cathedral, we need to appreciate why others have a different view. We need to walk around the
cathedral together, which is what we are doing in this book, walking
around the cathedral of Northern Ireland. But we also need to get
inside, to understand the point of the cathedral, the point of life
here.

Before we return, then, to my reflections on matters religious, let
me reiterate that a sense of perspective is important for those of us
living here. Lulled by our own television channels (for a population
less than 20% of London), deceived by English papers (which carry
different front pages for Northern Ireland), it is easy for us to think
that we are important to the outside world, or that we ought to be,
or that we can be if we only bomb our way into the news. But why
should others fret over our problems? The conflict in Northern
Ireland is not unique, nor is the scale of it as horrendous as in other
tragedies around the world. More people are dying in inter-tribal
fighting in South Africa in a week than have died in Northern
Ireland in a decade. People who live in any American city are six
times more likely to be killed violently than we are through our
Troubles. Three times as many people die here through car acci-
dents as through the Troubles yet there is precious little attention
devoted to the carnage on our roads. Please do not misunderstand
me. There is no acceptable minimum level of violence. But when,
as we recently learned, we hear that 6,000 people were killed in one
day by Lenin's troops, in one holy place, then we appreciate that
Northern Ireland cannot establish worldwide interest by trading

figures, nor by any escalation of any campaign of violence. What intrigues outsiders is not the level of violence but what seems to be the paradox of a religious conflict.

Even then, if you want to see a holy war, if you want to witness real interdenominational warfare, go to the Iran-Iraq border. And I suppose that on my academic travels, I have seen sights which do place Northern Ireland's problems in perspective. If you want to witness oppression, go to the concentration camps in Europe. In the summer before we came to Belfast, I visited Auschwitz in the company of philosophers including those who had themselves been prisoners in concentration camps. Soon after moving here, I spoke in Ashkabhad, on the border between the USSR and Iran, where communism, Russian Orthodoxy and Islam jostled for a hold over different ethnic groups. Going back a decade, I was living in Rome where I had the privilege of visiting the Mother Teresa nuns who worked in the shanty town (a rubbish tip) in the most appalling poverty on the outskirts of that most beautiful and prosperous city. In the preceding year, I had seen fear up and down the USA, in the Black ghetto only a few blocks from the White House, in prisons which were crammed with Hispanics and Blacks. Yale Law School is situated in a town which had far more frightening places than does the home of my present law school, Queen's. In Detroit, I visited a town whose murder rate is ten times that of any part of Northern Ireland. I was also, of course, able to see signs of hope in all these places, for instance the site in Detroit of Martin Luther King's first 'I had a dream' speech, later re-worked for the famous march on Washington DC.

I hope in a while to demonstrate the relevance of all this to your work. For now I will make two comments. First, we all have to make a spiritual journey, we are all on the road, as I shall argue later, the road to Emmaus. Second, what happens here in Northern Ireland can be affected by what happens elsewhere, a sense of perspective is much needed. No island is an island in itself.

All that was by way of refusing to apologise for being born outside Northern Ireland. Of course, it is open to insiders to dismiss outsiders but I would rather that you dismissed those outsiders who pander to the internal desire to be thought of as special. One of Churchill's worst contributions to Ireland was that dreadful quote about the integrity of the quarrel here. At the end of the First World War, you will remember, he said that everything in the world seemed to have changed except that we see what he called 'the dreary steeples of Fermanagh and Tyrone emerging once again. The integrity of their quarrel is one of the few institutions that have been left unaltered in the cataclysm which has swept the world'. Churchill was utterly wrong. Integrity is just what the quarrel lacks. The quote is brought out to depress those who think that if the Berlin Wall can be smashed then we can hope for the end of the conflict here. But Churchill's view of the cathedral, or at least the spires, of Northern Ireland, is so crucially myopic because Northern Ireland cannot resist the changing world. All is indeed in flux. If you think that the quarrel is about religions, then bear in mind that religions have changed since the myths took hold. If you claim it is about economic conditions, they too have changed. If it is about the idea that change only comes through violence, that ignores the available options of democracy which again have changed. If it is about media portrayal, they have changed, and indeed changed our lives through beaming a broader perspective into homes over the heads of teachers, clergies and parents. If you claim that the quarrel is about national identity, or political aspiration, or sovereignty, then bear in mind that sovereignty has changed in our European Community. The quarrel has changed. It has its own special features but it should not be viewed in splendid isolation.

A sense of perspective, then, tells me that the conflict here is not unique. But where it is *distinctive* is indeed in its religious element. Again, this is not unique. Only last week I was in Yorkshire, talking about the religious quarrel there in the wake of the Bradford Muslims' reaction to the Rushdie affair. In England, there has been a reluctance to admit that religion, rather than race, motivates discrimination. There has also been a reluctance to accept options other than the assimilation of minority cultures. In contrast, it is my belief that religion is the key element in understanding so much conflict in so many societies, from Bradford to Ballymena. Nor do I make any assumptions about the superiority of integrated over voluntarily separatist societies. But, I should add on that score that I have some doubts over the desire of ordinary people (as opposed to their self-appointed spokesmen) to live apart.

Again, from Bradford to Bangor, people will admit in private that an integrated workforce is what they desire and they recognise that it is difficult to achieve alongside segregated schooling, housing, socialising and religious practising.

If you will accept, at any rate, that I am portraying the cathedral of Northern Ireland from a different vantage point, which may show a different kind of light from the picture you have, then I have vindicated the right of an outsider to speak today. But why a lawyer? If the English have been viewed here with suspicion for centuries, academic lawyers have an even longer pedigree of being treated as pariahs. It was St Paul who captured the common view in his first letter to Timothy, chapter one, verse seven. (I have been told that there is no need to quote any Biblical passage, just cite it and everyone will know but, just in case it has slipped any minds, I will remind you that it reads: 'They have turned aside unto vain jangling, desiring to be teachers of the law, understanding neither what they say, nor whereof they affirm'). So why invite a vain jangler? I suppose that my interests, as a professor of jurisprudence or legal philosophy, cut across many disciplines, including philosophy, theology, sociology and politics. In my own work, I have been increasingly concerned with the impact of religion, or its lack of impact, on our lives. In my last book, *Believing Bishops* (Faber, 1990), my co-author and I at least predicted the name of the new Archbishop of Canterbury and we also like to think that we had something to say about the leadership of Anglican and Catholic churches (essentially, that a more prophetic role is needed). But rather than claim any religious credentials, beyond that of a Christian sinner, I think that I should accept that I have been invited simply in retaliation. Lawyers spend so much time listening to clerics here speaking on subjects about which they know very little, that it is time for a lawyer to be allowed to return the compliment by preaching a sermon.

So back to my roads out of town. Those who are understandably frightened by events here know, like the disciples who fled Jerusalem, that there is always a road to Emmaus, there is always a way out. There is the path of emigration, of secularisation, of alcohol, of drugs (medical and illegal) ... But after recognising Christ, His disciples turned back and faced the future in Jerusalem. I suggest that the examples of Martin Luther King and Mother Teresa might help scared Christians here face the future in faith.

The Mother Teresa story, pared to its essentials, is this. Each day, she sets out to see Christ in her neighbours. Whatever you do to the least of these my children, that you do unto me. The men of violence here say, ah, yes, Jesus, but I wouldn't be shooting you in the person of that policeman, this nun, those babies, those Australian lawyers in Holland, that man out shopping in Ardoyne, that lawyer in his home, that UDR soldier in his car, that man having a quiet drink in the pub, no Jesus I wouldn't be shooting you if only the Brits hadn't started it, or if only the republicans hadn't started it, if only, if only, if only ...

What does Mother Teresa say? She believes the Bible quite literally (in what critics call a fundamentalist way) when Jesus said that 'Whatever you do to the least of these, my children, that you do unto me' and she seeks to live her life accordingly. So each morning, she tries to see Jesus Christ (in some sense which you do not have to share) in the Eucharist. That communion gives her strength. Bear in mind that she feels a communion literally with those millions of people around the world who are doing the same every day. She believes that this helps her see Jesus in the dying and destitute people around her. Now, I would love to have time to argue about the finer points of transubstantiation but what needs to be stressed is rather the doctrine of *incarnation*. Christ *is* Risen. He *is* here. How should we behave towards Him? Whatever your religious denomination or faith. Mother Teresa has a message for you. I was debating against some law students earlier this year when one budding local politician asked, rhetorically, what would Christ say if He were here today? Points of order and information had been flowing throughout the debate so I raised what I called a point of religion and suggested that there was a theologically unsound use of the subjunctive in his question. Christ Is here. He is the one getting shot.

You will know that Mother Teresa won the Nobel Prize for Peace. You will also know that others resent that. Most recently, Germaine Greer wrote in The Independent about Mother Teresa as a villain, for a variety of reasons. At the time of her Nobel award, the oft-cited complaint was that she dealt with individuals to the exclusion of structures. Well, there is perhaps too much concentration here on structures and not enough on individuals. But I take the point. And so did Mother Teresa. She acknowledged the importance of tackling structural injustice but said that must be others' vocation.

Hence I have highlighted the work of another Nobel Laureate, Martin Luther King, who *did* work in that way. He had a dream. Again, a dream inspired by the Gospels. It was a dream for a different land, of course, but one which passes the test of time and which transcends its American context. There are three speeches by Dr King which should haunt us here, especially those who purport to share the Reverend King's brand of Christianity. His speech at the March on Washington closed in this way.

'When we let freedom ring ... we will be able to speed up that day when all God's children, black men and white men, Jews and gentiles, Protestants and Catholics, will be able to joint hands and sing in the words of that old Negro spiritual, "Free at last! Free at last! Thank God almighty, we are free at last".'

Second, he seemed to have a premonition of his assassination when he said, only hours before he died:

'I've been to the mountaintop ... And I've looked over, and I've seen the promised land [lest any Unionists start calling him a Lundy, by mountaintop, he was not referring to the Mournes and by the promised land, he was not referring to the Republic]. I may not get there with you but I want you to know tonight that we as a people will get to the promised land. So I'm happy tonight. I'm not fearing any man. Mine eyes hath seen the glory of the coming of the Lord.'

Once he had conquered fear, his work was done and he died violently, but at peace with his Lord.

Third, Martin Luther King gave us food for thought in *his* Nobel acceptance speech, in a passage with which I close my book, *The Cost of Free Speech*, a passage which I find deeply moving:

'I have the audacity to believe [that is what we need here in Northern Ireland, the audacity to believe] that peoples every–where can have three meals a day for their bodies, education and culture for their minds, and dignity, equality and freedom for their spirits. I believe that what self-centered men have torn down, other-centered can build up. I still believe that one day mankind will bow before the altars of God and be crowned triumphant over war and bloodshed, and nonviolent re-demption goodwill will proclaim the rule of the land. And the lion and the lamb shall lie down together and every man shall sit under his own fig tree and none shall be afraid. I still believe that we shall overcome.'

I have called to mind two great modern examplars of Christian love and life. Let me now refer you to two great stories from the Gospel, the message of Christ which has so informed the lives of Mother Teresa and Martin Luther King. Let's think of those two roads out of Jerusalem, to Jericho and Emmaus. First, the road to Jericho.

It was, you will recall, a mere lawyer who asked Jesus to explain who was his neighbour and who prompted the story of the Good

Samaritan on the road to Jericho. Martin Luther King once preached a powerful sermon about this, having visited the scene of the story and seen what a dangerous road it was, a steep descent from Jerusalem, full of twists and turns, ideal bandit country. In a sermon, he once asked why the priest and Levite didn't stop and answered, more or less, that they might have been rushing to an ecumenical talking-shop at Cookstown. Or, he added, most likely they were scared. Perhaps, said Martin Luther King in words which anticipated our experiences, they thought the body was a booby-trapped dummy.

The priest's first question, hypothesised Dr King, was 'If I stop to help this man, what will happen to me?' The Samaritan's was 'If I do not stop, what will happen to him?' Too often, priests here ask 'what will my parishioners/parish priest/governors/teachers/bishops say if I agree to visit the integrated school, the state school, the minister, the police, the UDR?' Too often ministers here think 'what will happen to my job, my home, my family, if I join that ecumenical prayer-group, if I go to Clonard, if I attend that Catholic funeral?' And I know that those who had the altruism of the Good Samaritan have had to pay the price, congregations have forced out Christian Ministers who have dared to take Christ at His word. I know also that so many religious people, on all sides, have been Good Samaritans risking their own lives to give comfort to the dying person that might indeed be a booby-trapped body on a border road. Nor do I condemn those priests who walk by on the other side, or who are too fearful to open their doors to help the Christ outside. But I do say that we, as a people, as the people of God, need to build up our faith to the point where individuals have the strength that comes from freedom from fear, to behave like Good Samaritans. Amid depressing news, there are always signs of hope. How wonderful to see last week that an inter-community group FAIT, has begun to act as Good Samaritans to protect the Good Samaritans themselves who have been brave enough to summon help by dialling 999.

What of the road to Emmaus? How astonishing that the disciples did not recognise Jesus. Or was it? It takes a Mother Teresa to recognise Jesus in the leper on the streets of Bombay, or in the person of a paramilitary. So what was it which led to the scales falling from the disciples' eyes? What gave them freedom from the fear which blighted their lives, again understandably? Something stirred when He began to explain the scriptures to them. That led them to ask Him to stay. Once they had *given*, in that little way, they recog-nised Him in the breaking of bread. This does not necessarily imply a Eucharist, although Mother Teresa might gain spiritual strength from thinking in those terms. Perhaps it was simply that they recognised the way in which He acted, because they were familiar with His movements. But it was at least in sharing that most basic of activities, eating, that they found the courage to return to face a turbulent Jerusalem. If people in Northern Ireland, like those at this conference today, can act together in any way whatsoever, *we* will find it easier to see the Christ in one another.

How can church leaders facilitate all this? First, by urging their fellow Christians never to do alone what can be done together. This is easier said than done, but it is easier done in Christ than avoided in fear. Church unity services should follow where charity work, education for mutual understanding, day trips for senior citizens, and other practical activities, have led. Second, church leaders should indeed lead by example. If we cannot yet have joint services, or even joint initiatives, we can at least have joint statements, of condemnation but also of praise. It should not be beyond the wit of leaders to organise joint statements so that after every outrage we hear on the news, 'Church leaders united to express sympathy to A, B, C and to issue a strong denunciation XYZ'. More positively, how nice it would be to hear 'Church leaders united to exhort all men and women of goodwill to work across denominational divides in their charitable works'.

But I began by reminding you that *we* are the Churches. Even where church leaders are slow to act as one, *we* should act for progress anyway. Never do alone what can be done together is the message of hope from around the world. It is in doing the little things together that we begin to conquer fear. In the USSR, there has been an awesome underground struggle to keep Christian faith alive in circumstances where the luxury of inter-denominational disputes could not be allowed to interfere with spreading the Gospel message. In what seem to be easier circumstances, such as elsewhere in these islands, I hear time and again religious leaders telling me that they feel more at home with people of other faiths than with the growing tide of secularism. The Rushdie saga has spawned amazing alliances, little groups of Muslims, Christians, Jews, Hindus, Sikhs, and Buddhists exploring ways in which they can work together, as well as recognising when they feel more comfortable apart.

So what kinds of practical co-operation do I have in mind, here in Northern Ireland?

The CCCCW has focused on one issue which might seem a

strange starting-point but which I think shows how inspired (literally) they are: the question of emigration of young people to higher education elsewhere. The future of Northern Ireland is bleak if talented leaders leave at 18, to return only as visitors rather than as residents. In particular, I know full well that many parents whose children attend state grammar schools expect them to pursue their studies across the water. I am fascinated to hear their explanations for this when they learn that I am at Queen's.

I should add that although there are more Catholics in England than in the whole island of Ireland, the assumption of many Northern Irish folk is that anyone with an English accent, other than Basil Hume, is a Protestant. This is as mistaken as the image that the English parade the Union Jack or take every opportunity to play the national anthem. It relates, if at all, to the England of a bygone age. There are, of course, more practising Muslims than Anglicans in England, almost as many Buddhists as Baptists, as many Jews as Methodists. But still, if people think that I am a Protestant, they sometimes confide that the reason why Protestant children go away is because 'the republicans' have taken over the students' union. By which is meant, I think, that there are a few signs in Irish. In fact, the reason why the children want to get away is because they don't want to live at home, quite understandably. Don't blame the Troubles, although they contribute. Don't blame ourselves. Don't blame Queen's. It is true of young people everywhere in the world - they want to assert their independence. It is as true of Catholics as Protestants here. It is as true of Northerners in England who like to go to college in the South, and Southerners who move North. There is no need to deceive ourselves into thinking otherwise. Of course, some will stay (especially given poll tax and student loans) for financial reasons (just as some youngsters attend local universities in the USA) and some will stay because the local universities excel in many ways. Those who go will meet future spouses and employers and may well not return. So what?

So the local universities must attract people from outside the North, which they are doing. From your perspective, they must also work harder to attract local students. My own view is that we should offer more and more degrees which build in time away from Northern Ireland (eg our joint law degree with Louvain in Belgium) so that students get that sense of distance, adventure, freedom, while expecting to return. Indeed, if I had any power (which I do not) I would lay down a requirement of taking students away for at least a term as my objective for Northern Irish universities in all their degrees. I think that the inevitable trend for UK universities is to allow terms at other institutions, both within and without the UK, so that may lead us in that direction anyway.

Meanwhile you can share the fears of emigration, and also its opportunities (eg to visit new places, perhaps to question your assumptions about the English and their assumptions about you). As this committee's research has shown, *both* communities share the fear of emigration. Both have an interest in replacing the Liverpool ferry, just as both have an interest in keeping the Dublin train line free for travel. If coming to terms with emigration is a problem, then the fear of our children moving away is one which pastoral work can help conquer.

Let me take another issue, a more controversial one: primary and secondary education. My own experience of making the mildest comments in support of trying another alternative way forward, integrated education, is that some Catholic clergy here are petrified by the fear of losing the power-base of their schools. It saddens me that some fellow Catholics can write with a lack of Christian charity about integrated schools which they will not even visit. But I live in hope that we can revocer the spirit of the Catholic Bishop of Kildare and Leighlin, Dr Doyle, who said in the middle of the nineteenth century: 'I do not know of any measures which would prepare the way for a better feeling in Ireland, than uniting children at an early age and bringing them up in the same school, leading them to commune with one another and to form these little intimacies and friendships which often subsist through life.'

The fear of losing control in that one area of life where Catholics have always felt secure, through the Stormont years, that fear is paralysing. If it were to be lifted, other fears would come to the fore, the fear of some Protestant parents who feel equally uneasy with the idea of this committee's history project. On all sides, we see again the fear of change. In 1988, a working party of the churches of Britain and Ireland declared that it 'believed that integrated schools have significant potential for the healing of community divisions and that they deserve the fullest support of the Churches and the secular authorities. In particular, the Churches should not delay in setting up chaplaincies at these schools, to provide pastoral care for staff and pupils'. What has happened to that recommendation? On the other hand, a word of praise is surely appropriate for all those who, while they cannot yet find it in themselves to be open to the possibilities of integrated education, have co-operated in what I would call the quest for integrity-in-education and which is officially called Education for Mutual Understanding.

Let me take a third area of life here, the media. Journalists do a wonderful job of beaming into our homes, over the heads of those clergy and teachers and parents who live in the past, the full range of ideas bubbling in the wider world, a world of many faiths and of none. The government feels, to judge by what an English judge called its half-baked media restrictions on the supporters of violence, that television confers a legitimacy on those it broadcasts. If so, then television and radio must turn to report the Good News of reconciliation in Northern Ireland. But I wonder whether a slightly dated society does not still place more trust in what appears in print. There must be a place for a well-produced inter-church magazine, taking advantage of desk-top publishing possibilities and an unrivalled distribution network (ie the church porch) to debate the successes and failures of your steps towards co-operation.

There are so many areas of life where fear crosses denominational or community divides and where good work is being done: comforting the bereaved, protecting the intimidated, strengthening the family. It may well be that the churches have not done enough to implement the 1976 report, Violence in Ireland, in which you will recall the recommendation that 'the churches actively support peace and reconciliation movements'. But the work has begun. And I am well aware that the work is being done in different ways all over Northern Ireland.

The view from Derry is not the same as that from Omagh, nor from Armagh. I look forward to hearing about your different experiences shortly. But before I close, let me indulge in what I regard as a digression but which I know others are waiting to hear about. Is there a political angle to all this?

My interest in the churches' work is that I hope we can help one another to live out the Gospel message. Of course, I am well aware that much of the interest in a conference like this, or in your inter-community work, has a different motivation - others are interested because it might help the political climate. If that happens, then all well and good, but it is not *our* primary purpose. Nevertheless, if a spirit of freedom from fear were to take hold, what impact might that have?

Of course Christ would talk about talks about talks. The fact that it is so difficult to get our politicians to the conference table, however, is a reflection of their constituents' fear. That is the tragedy of Northern Ireland: the fear of reaching out, of going the extra mile. It is that fear which blights so many lives here. Freedom from that fear would not only facilitate talks about talks in the political sense, it would make them almost unnecessary. I do not wish to make any further comment today on our political scene. But I will simply quote a theologian whose work is wonderfully poised on the cusp between Catholicism and Protestantism (or perhaps whose work denies that there is any great divide). Hans Kung has noted that in disputes such as ours (although he was not talking about Northern Ireland), both sides have rights, both sides can back up their claims to rights. But, he argues in 'On Being A Christian':

> 'the Christian message [says] that renouncing rights without expecting anything in return is not necessarily a disgrace: that Christians at least should not despise a politician who is prepared to make concessions ... a renunciation of rights without recompense can constitute the great freedom of the Christian: he is going two miles with someone who has forced him to go one. The Christian who lives in this freedom becomes critical of all those - on whatever side - who constantly protest verbally their peaceful intentions, who are always promising friendship and reconciliation for the sake of propaganda, but in practical politics are not prepared for the sake of peace occasionally to give up obsolete legal positions, to take a first step towards the other person, publicly to struggle for friendship with other[s ...] even when this is unpopular.'

In that spirit, in our personal lives more importantly than in our leaders' political lives, let's turn back from the road to Emmaus. Let's go two miles back towards Jerusalem, with one another, with the Christ we have finally recognised in one another. I, for one, have the audacity to believe, with Martin Luther King, that nonviolent redemptive goodwill will triumph, that mankind will bow down before God, that none shall be afraid, that we shall overcome.

PART III

PRESENTATIONS BY INTER-CHURCH
COMMUNITY GROUPS

THE CHURCHES' ROLE IN COMMUNITY RELATIONS

Rev. Tom Craig

People from various places in Northern Ireland have been asked to share with us what they have been doing. What some of us have thought about in a tentative fashion they have actually put into practice. The proposition that we might work inter-church for the benefit of our own local community is no longer theoretical. It is being done daily by 'ordinary' people.

The speakers are as follows:

The Rev Sam Burch is a Methodist minister, seconded to the Cornerstone Community, which is based on inter-church prayer. This group has developed over the years a ministry of pastoral care to the families of victims of the 'Troubles'. I can speak of my own experience of this pastoral care to one of the families of my former congregation, and how appreciatively it was received.

The Rev Julian McCready, curate, Seagoe Parish, and Miss Esther Elliott, co-ordinator for the Killicomaine Care Project will speak in place of the Rev David Chillingworth, detained by parish duties. This group arose out of the tensions and aftermath of the Anglo-Irish Treaty protests and out of the realisation by local churches of the many problems faced by people living in the area. In their situation they have had to face right wing opposition from the Protestant side, even though the Project had to be of necessity entirely Protestant.

Mr Michael McCooe is from the Drumcree Faith and Justice group. They work in an exclusively Roman Catholic area in Portadown and found great difficulty in making contact with working class Protestant groups.

Mr Martin McCrystal comes from Project Portadown, an ACE scheme which made a break through by bringing Protestants and Catholics together in the same work teams. It illustrated the importance many placed on having a job, which overcame many other factors.

Mr Robin Toner is the full time Development Officer for the Barnabas Trust, Enniskillen. This Trust started as a Methodist outreach, but now has an inter-church Committee of Reference.

Mr Matt Patterson is the current Chairman of the Co-Leck Care, Leckpatrick. This group has a special place in my esteem, not only for what they are doing but because of the way the group originated.

Mr Ivan Webb, full-time Development Officer for the New Mossely Community Project. This group illustrates the need for patience in inter-church and community work. They were together for eight years before their work began to develop to its present level.

THE CORNERSTONE COMMUNITY

The Cornerstone Community is a group of around 16 people, mainly from the four major denominations, Roman Catholic, Church of Ireland, Presbyterian and Methodist, but usually with some folk from the smaller denominations like Quakers, Lutherans etc.

We came together as a Community in 1983, following a long period of around seven years exploring our common Faith and Christian experience in a Prayer Group at Clonard Monastery.

The pressure which impelled us towards Community was the polarization of the Falls-Shankill communities, the escalating violence and in particular the fears and hostility aroused in these areas by the hunger strike. We feared a slide into civil war or at least a critical escalation of the violence and a hardening of the apartheid of the communities into mutual fear and hostility which would be very difficult to overcome. This anxiety led the Clonard Prayer Group to ask itself if there was anything more we could do in this situation. Our response was to form the Community with fifteen of the twenty-five members of the Prayer Group committing themselves by a spiritual covenant to each other, to a weekly meeting and a common meal and to support each other by prayer and practice in our desire for reconciliation in this area. Five of the fifteen members agreed to leave their own homes and come together into a community house in order to be a core for the whole Community.

We believe our calling to be, to work for peace and reconciliation, especially in the Falls-Shankill area of West Belfast and we seek to to this in a number of ways.

1. By being a symbol of unity and a sign of hope. Our presence as Catholics and Protestants living together in a completely polarised area is itself a powerful statement and a challenge to those around not to accept the walls of division as right or permanent. So the house is a place of welcome for all who want to leave their labels and meet as equals and celebrate the joy of life and relationships.

2.   A Community of Prayer. We continually pray and offer oppor-
     tunity for joint prayer for the area and especially for those
     suffering because of the violence. Our belief is that this is the
     most important and effective work we can do for our area. We
     have seen those, hurt and broken by their experiences in the
     violence, healed and restored and we have witnessed great
     changes in people and in the environment. We are sure that
     spiritual forces are being released through prayer that will make
     significant changes possible in the future.

3.   By exercising a wide range of ministries and services in and for
     the local community, which we feel will be helpful in promoting
     peace and better relations. These are both proactive and reactive.
     For instance on the 31 July, John Judge was shot dead in a street
     just off the Springfield Road. Immediately members of the
     Community both Catholic and Protestant visited the home and
     comforted the family. We have continued to visit and a month
     after the shooting held an act of worship and prayer at the spot,
     when, around 50 Protestant and Catholic people gathered to
     affirm the sacredness of life and the call of the Gospel to love
     and to cherish one another. We try to react positively to the
     negative things that happen around us and challenge others to
     do the same. We also plan and promote activities that will help
     to break down barriers and foster better relations. Thus we run
     a Clergy and Church Workers Fellowship; a Youth Leaders
     Fellowship; an After Schools Club and a healing service at which
     Protestants and Catholics meet and share.
        Because of the tribal fears and hatred in the area it can be
     difficult and indeed dangerous to move out in goodwill to the
     'other side'. We have found it helpful for members of the
     Community to move into sectors and activities of the 'other
     side'. So a protestant member will share in worship and service
     in a catholic neighbourhood and vice versa
        We have found how important symbolic action can be even if
     it is something quite small. Catholic members presented flow-
     ers to Protestant congregations in the Shankill and Protestant
     clergy in uniform attended funerals of Catholic victims murdered
     in the violence.
        Two years ago we organised a 'Way of the Cross' walk which
     surprised us in the impact in made both on the community and
     on those who walked. It occurred just after the series of killings

following the Gibraltar shootings when emotions were running very high. 1500 people came and prayed and carried a 14 foot cross from the Falls end of the Springfield Road through the ugly symbol of the so called 'Peace Wall' up to the park at the top of the Shankill Road. There was a very hostile reaction to this from a small crowd on the Shankill Road, but most of the people along the route were supportive. Gestures like this may seem futile in that they have little or no effect on the people of violence or their hard line supporters but the community at large needs to be continually encouraged and reinforced in their will to achieve peace and good relationships.

One of the roles that has given us much joy and has been very enriching in our mission is to be host to young people from many parts of the world, who have wanted to come and help in a challenging situation. We have had Americans, Canadians, Scandinavians and Europeans, some of whom have made considerable sacrifices to be part of our mission. It has been inspirational to see their enthusiasm and commitment and it makes us wonder if part of our problem is that we are not providing opportunities enough for our own young people to face demanding and soul stretching challenges.

Difficulties

In all of this work for reconciliation and peace, we struggle against major difficulties.

1. There is the inertia of the local communities who have settled in their minds that the divisions in our society are permanent and irreconcilable. This is the way it has always been and will always be. There is nothing any of us can do to make any significant change. They wish the other side would change but make little or no effort to change themselves. One of the factors in this inertia is the low level of violence. Most people can live with only minor discomfort and disruption to their lives. They regret the deaths and injuries but have learned to live with them - like road deaths, so there is no compelling pressure to change or accommodate.

    The churches very largely share this inertia. They are either trapped in the sectarianism and have become part of the tribal fear and hostility or they desire reconciliation but not enough to make any significant changes in their agendas or commit money or manpower to it. Apart from trying to improve their own relationships - what one of our members calls "salon ecumenism" - as churches they have done little enough to stem the tide of secularism and sectarianism that is devastating both communities.

With most other voluntary groups we share the frustration of lack of money and personnel. Most of our members are busy, heavily committed community or church workers with little time or energy outside of this. While they welcome the stimulus of the Community and the exchange of views and heroically try to live and work it out in their homes and jobs they can not give a lot of time and effort specifically to this work. Those who make it a full time commitment feel at times like King Canute trying to stop the tide coming in.

Financially we operate on a very tight budget which leaves little scope for venture and experiment. Nevertheless, within these constraints and in spite of the difficulties, we believe that we have made a significant hole in the dividing wall that separates the Shankill and the Falls and we are confident that its days are numbered. We believe that more and more people will follow our example because they see it as right and possible and I am sure they will be more effective in the way they will tackle it. We are glad to have been able to make a start and to have encouraged others to work for peace in this troubled area of Belfast.

THE CORNERSTONE COMMUNITY
443/445 Springfield Road
Belfast BT12 7DL
Tel (0232) 321649

KILLICOMAINE CARING GROUP

Who are we?

Killicomaine Caring Group is two years old. The Group is sponsored by four local Churches, First Portadown Presbyterian Church, Edenderry Methodist Church, Killicomaine Evangelical Church and Seagoe Parish Church.

We are committed to working together with the local community to develop programmes in Killicomaine Estate, Portadown. This is a large housing area in East Portadown, now almost entirely Protestant, with widespread social need among young people, young families, particularly single parent families, and the elderly.

Why did we start up?

Our movement towards working together began with a concern about the level of under-age drinking in the area - we gradually became aware of wider needs and also of the relative ineffectiveness of any of our Churches working alone in meeting these needs.

We resolved to form a Management Committee drawn from our Churches and from the community and to develop a programme of community action.

We remain committed to our work together in the area. It has certainly helped to develop relationships of friendship and trust among the clergy involved and our people see this as a natural way in which Churches should work.

There is no Roman Catholic population in the estate and no Roman Catholic parish organisation to which we can effectively relate.

What have we done?

1. *Management* - We formed a Management Committee.

2. *Premises* - We acquired two maisonettes from the NIHE at a nominal rent.

3. *Groups* - We established the following groups: Senior Citizens; Mother & Toddler; After School Group. We also established a simple Advice Centre and our premises are also used by a local Parents Group involved in special tuition for children with learning difficulties.

4. *ACE Programme* - We employ ACE Workers (8) initially through ACE Ventures and now through Project Portadown. The workers run a major environmental programme in the area and support volunteers in running the programme.

5. *Volunteers* - We have recruited volunteers from our Churches and the community to staff the Centre.

What have we received?

We have received help from:

- our churches
- NIHE for premises
- SHSSB in grant aid and other support
- Craigavon Borough Council
- Charitable Trusts

We were surprised and disappointed by the inability of CCCCW to offer us help, although we were grateful for the time and encouragement given to us by the Chairman.

What problems have we had?

What lessons can we share?

Our problems have been almost entirely those of staffing. An organisation of this kind needs full-time development work at the centre if volunteers are to be encouraged to become involved and develop their skills.

ACE employment is a valuable asset but it cannot meet this need.

We believe that we shall have to look again at where we are going and work out how best Killicomaine Caring Group can develop. We

are very encouraged by what has been accomplished but we believe
that we are only touching the surface in terms of the needs and the
potential.

KILLICOMAINE CARING GROUP
65 Seagoe Road
Portadown BT63 5HS
Tel: (0762) 350583

DRUMCREE FAITH AND JUSTICE GROUP

The Drumcree Faith and Justice are a group of people who are drawn from the community that lives along the Garvaghy Road in Portadown. The group came together after a public meeting in July 1985. At the time there were riots every night. The cause of the riots was that the annual Orange Church parade was due that Sunday. The area had been saturated with security forces. This happened every year and normal daily life was impossible.

Harassment by the security forces of the residents did not help the situation and restrictions on normal life (if any life in Northern Ireland is normal) became intolerable.

A group of concerned residents came together and decided they would hold a public meeting. The reasons for doing this were many but the uppermost in people's minds was to put an end to the rioting before someone was killed. This fear was expressed at the meeting and it decided on a course of non-violence for three reasons:

1. We all resented the restrictions on daily life which were imposed two weeks before these parades.

2. The parade itself was not welcome in the area and non-violent protest concentrated on it would show better than a riot what the actual problem was.

3. You cannot reasonably expect someone to listen to your point of view if you insist on trying to hurt/kill them.

In this case we wanted to put our point of view to the security forces at whom the young people were throwing stones and petrol bombs. These were the only people in our opinion who could stop these parades.

The people who volunteered for membership of the group at the public meeting also decided the group should be cross community. They felt that only the growth of respectful relationships between

Catholics and Protestants in their church hall, etc., and in our community centre to try and tease out an answer to our problems in Portadown, parades after all were only one issue. Many others needed to be faced and the only way to do this was to talk directly to each other. We also attended Protestant services and they attended ours. The ultimate goal was to learn about each other since ignorance lends itself to all sorts of myths.

During 1985/6 the group continued to build relations in the 'other community' with the result that meetings were taking place on a monthly basis in different venues. However, in 1987 we found that the parade was coming again. After a lot of soul searching we decided to hold a tea party on the middle of Garvaghy Road. Not so much to protest but to bear witness to what we saw as an injustice. Another aspect of the tea party was that Protestants had also agreed to sit at the table to show how Protestants and Catholics can get on together when they treat each other with respect. We displayed placards asking for equality, respect, justice, etc. The tea party is now an annual event. Two years ago the group decided to step up its action and hold a sit-down protest. Only group members took part in this and only those who agreed to. There was no pressure from other group members. This was a personal choice. The decision to do this was not taken lightly. The group discussed at length the problems involved, not least was the question - is it fair to put the RUC in a position where they would have to lift us off the road? Last year the group decided to hold an anniversary/peace parade. The route chosen was exactly the same as the one the Orangemen use on the Sunday before the Twelfth. After all, the Chief Constable had described this rout as an open thoroughfare. After the initial 7 day notice had been given we were called to a meeting the following Wednesday in the Police Station with the Operations Commander of the RUC. Various alternatives were offered, none of which included the Town Centre (Catholics have never been allowed to march in Portadown town centre). They were considered unsatisfactory by the group. Another thing about this meeting was that the commander had neglected to mention that the group had received death threats from the Protestant Action Force. The group was aware of this because the Portadown Times had a telephone call from someone representing this group and using a recognised codeword on Monday. We found out because they rang for a comment. We were summoned again to a meeting on Friday afternoon at 3.30 pm (the parade was due to get underway at 7.00 pm). Mrs Anna Fowler and I as organisers were handed banning orders which banned us and our group from every street in Portadown except for 400 yards along Garvaghy Road. The reason given for this was that while we ourselves would not cause public disorder our very presence was likely to lead to serious public disorder, particularly in view of the threat from the PAF.

While it may seem to many of you that we only tackle issues such as parades, this is not true. In May this year the Provisional IRA threatened two young men from Churchill Park with death if they did not leave Northern Ireland by Thursday of that week. The threat was made on Monday. The Group heard of this and decided that something should be done. We asked all the usual questions such as who were these people to decide what was anti-social behaviour? After all they killed people - was that not anti-social? What gave them the right to judge others? What defence, if any, had been put for these young men? We decided we would hold a poll of the estate to see if the residents agreed with the IRA. The aforementioned questions were asked, and we got a resounding 'No' from the residents. These people said the IRA did not have the right to do this. We presented our results to Sinn Fein and publicised them on radio and in the press. The two young men still had to go. Our negotiations were unsuccessful. But we fell that the IRA will think twice before they try anything like this in future, because our poll showed them that they had no community support for their actions.

One of the main problems a group such as ours experiences is mistrust. Another problem is that we are seen as well meaning people who are to be congratulated on what we are trying to achieve but we are not really taken seriously. The first problem of mistrust comes from the old Northern Irish disease of labelling people as either Nationalist or Unionist. This happens because of the issues a group such as ours deals with. For example, we as a group meet Protestants to try and reach a mutual understanding of each other's points of view. We negotiate with the police about the problem. We have even been asked by the RUC in times of previous public disorder to calm the area down (which we have done). yet we are seen in many Protestant eyes as a Nationalist group who wish only to take away what they see as their British right. The second problem can only be solved with time and a lot of hard work.

The lessons to be learned from all this are that small cross-community groups have a very limited field of operation. For example, it has been our experience that to get to talk to working class Protestants is almost impossible. Only people who have met our group on numerous occasions understand our position fully. When any group in Northern Ireland attempts to step out of the circle of myths that we have about each other they must be prepared to work hard at getting their real message across. Misunderstanding and misrepresentation of actions taken, particularly those that are reported in the press, lead to all sorts of difficulties after times of tension in Northern Ireland. The group's credibility has suffered serious blows on numerous occasions due to this.

DRUMCREE FAITH AND JUSTICE GROUP
c/o 'Iona'
221 Churchill Park
Portadown
BT62 1EU

Tel: (0752) 330366

PROJECT PORTADOWN

For some years now two ACE groups have been operating within the Portadown area. One was being run by the Killicomaine Caring Group and serviced the needs of the Protestant people in the adjoining housing estates; the other was being run by a group called the Drumcree Community Education Project and operated in the Catholic area of Portadown. While the work carried out by these groups was certainly of community benefit it was felt by those involved that the area of cross community relations was being neglected.

On the 4th June of this year the two ACE groups amalgamated and Project Portadown came into being. The organisation has five broad aims:

1. To offer help to the needy in the community especially the elderly, disabled, and single parents without distinction of age or religion.

2. To enhance peace and reconciliation within the area of Portadown and neighbouring townlands.

3. To operate a Job Creation Programme for the benefit of the long term unemployed.

4. To assist social deviants ie ex-offenders or possible offenders and to rehabilitate them into society.

5. To increase the commitment to voluntary action in the Portadown area. In order to achieve these aims we are involved in a number of areas of work. These include:
   (a) A Community Education Programme.
   (b) A gardening and home decorating service provided for the elderly and other disadvantaged groups.
   (c) A local History Project.

(d) A home visitation service for pensioners.
(e) Welfare Rights advice.
(f) A Conservation Project.
(g) Involvement in a Community Newspaper.

We have come together in order to enable people from both sections of the community to work together and through this contact to realise that they are basically the same, sharing similar day to day difficulties. Hopefully this contact will instil some level of mutual respect for each other and will give an indication to the worker that it is possible to live together in a harmonious manner. We also hope that these feelings will spill over into the community where we carry out our work. Even though our group has only been in existence for a short time we are already learning from our experiences. The first problem that we faced was that our workers were reluctant to go into areas dominated by numbers of the opposite persuasion. We have not been able to overcome this 'Ghetto mentality' and would indeed agree that it is too big a step to take at this early stage. However, we were pleasantly surprised to discover that none of our workers had any objection to working together in a central and mixed area of the town. We are also using the area of training a a vehicle for mixing our work force and see this as our first major step to building up cross community relations within the project. We realise that we are only a small group trying to tackle a major problem but hope that our efforts mixed with those of other similar groups will help to change present attitudes.

PROJECT PORTADOWN
28 William Street
Portadown BT62 3NX

Tel (0762) 350665

THE BARNABAS TRUST

The Barnabas Message

The work of the Trust today and the opportunities of tomorrow have been made possible because we believe the Gospel message contains the call to serve others in the name of Christ. We are all called to this work and we are called to serve everyone. The services the Barnabas Trust provide and the mechanism we use are not unique or exclusive. If anything makes us special it is the way God as blessed us and the way prayers have been answered. Perhaps our message might be made clearer if these prayer requests were shared.

Community

We prayed that people would be drawn closer to Christ and closer to each other through their involvement in this work. The desire and need to help others has given people an opportunity to examine what is really important and to work together to achieve it.

Hope

We prayed that people might be encouraged through the assistance we are able to give them in their difficulties. We have learnt that Paul's words in Romans 5 are still true - tribulation can create patience, and experience of suffering can bring hope. Sometimes all it needs is someone to listen.

Resources

We prayed for all the resources necessary for the work. We were encouraged to find many statutory and voluntary bodies willing to advise, support and finance our activities. We have not always received positive answers to every request but have not been discouraged and have often been referred to another source of help. In fact the 'networking' with other organisations involved in similar work has been most encouraging.

Individuals

We prayed that individuals might be changed through assisting with problems greater than their own. In their exposure to deferent experiences and attitudes they have overcome helpless uncertainty and nameless doubt and the certainty of their faith has been established and confirmed.

Staff

We prayed for success in recruitment that the knowledge, skills and attitudes of the applicants would meet the needs of the work. The continuing professionalism of our staff, who now represent the third 'team' we have recruited, owes much to the selection of Mrs Sylvia Lucy as manager. The development of individual members of staff as a result of their employment has itself been one of our success stories.

Trust

We prayed expectantly with assurance that, whatever happened, the idea of Barnabas would somehow be translated into action. After only three years it is frightening to realise how many of those prayers have been answered. It is not because we didn't make mistakes. It is because we were bold enough to ask the Lord and having asked we believed that we had received.

The Barnabas Centre

The success of the Trust's work to date has exposed the urgency for more initiatives to tackle the social problems which need to be addressed by the expansion of planned programmes of care. To date this has been restricted by lack of space and a suitable environment.

This obstacle has now been overcome by the purchase of the 'Old Library Building' which has been made possible by the generous assistance of the Department of Education.

The advantages of a large building with main street frontage and in a central location in the town will facilitate the Trust's initiatives in the following ventures:

Youth

The creation in the basement area of a properly equipped and professionally managed 'Pub with no Beer' with traditional character and attractive amenities will be a facility which will draw young people onto our premises. Staff will dispense non-alcoholic drinks and food and encourage participation in recreation and use will be made of an open area for dancing, drama and displays. Involvement in these and other club activities will help develop a team spirit of co-operation. A youth leader will encourage participation in self-development and community awareness programme.

Enterprise

A commercial restaurant will serve the general public, the business community, the tourist sector and the clubs and will give employment and enterprise experience.

Day Centre

In addition to our present club activities we plan to use the facilities for: a library of special toys for children with learning difficulties; a special club for those suffering from depression and mental illness; a wellwoman club to encourage and assist mothers in child care and home management; a jobsearch club to utilise the skills and experience of the elderly members of our day clubs to help the unemployed. A quiet room will be available for counselling those who need help.

Accommodation

Provision of 5 short stay units adapted to suite the handicapped will assist those returning to the community from institutional care or those who have similar temporary housing difficulties.

In the beginning ...

The name of Barnabas in the New Testament is linked with practical help and hard work. It means 'Son of Encouragement' which is what the Trust is giving to people of Fermanagh. It arose from the concern expressed by the Methodist people of Enniskillen for the particular problems of their district.

This is an extensive rural area with transport and communication difficulties which have a significant effect on the lives of those who are forced to stay at home because of infirmity or age. Analysis of the population shows 16% over the age of 65. The number of large employers has reduced in recent years and there are few natural resources or indigenous skills to provide a strong economic base. Dairy and store cattle which were the traditional farming base are also suffering a severe economic recession. Consequently the lack of opportunities for young people has increased unemployment rates to almost 20%, and in turn this has led to increasing rates of migration by young people and has inevitably reduced the support base of carers for these older members of the community.

In 1987 this concern was stimulated by the appointment to the circuit of the Rev Derrick Haskins, who had experience of a community caring project in a previous post. As these hopes and concerns were raised in prayer the vision became clearer. Then later the tragic consequences of the Remembrance Day Bomb not only highlighted the needs previously identified but also demanded a positive response as a witness of Christianity.

The work began in June 1988 with the recruitment of a full time manager and nineteen workers funded by the Department of the Economic Development through the Action for Community Employment (ACE) scheme, which is the local equivalent of the former Employment Training Scheme of the Manpower Services Commission. Charitable status was recognised in June 1989 and in January 1990 representatives of the four main Churches in Enniskillen met together to form the Inter-Church Council of Reference to advise, review, comment and report on the work being done. A Board of Trustees was appointed by them and the Trust Deed was executed in March 1990. Currently we are responsible for 43 ACE posts and receive help from 10 other volunteers on a regular basis.

Present Operations

We currently provide the following services:

Renewing
Our environmental care team assist in redecorating homes and

maintaining gardens of those who are no longer able to do this for themselves. We are therefore able to foster pride in appearance and community spirit. Some 200 homes have been redecorated in the current year and 400 gardening projects completed.

Restoring

Our visitation team have extended their befriending to 160 homes every week. Through this regular contact they are helping those who are isolated by age or infirmity to relate to the rest of the community. Practical help and advice is also given in conjunction with other caring agencies and respite sitting is also offered.

Our pre-school playgroup is helping children with special needs to relate to the world around them and is also encouraging their development. It also provides necessary respite for parents.

Our installation service for Lifeline Telephones provided through Help the Aged has been a vital link for those who may need urgent assistance and be otherwise unable to call for it.

Revitalising

Our club activities programme is providing a focus for the 100 members who, for reasons of age of infirmity, need assistance to meet together to enjoy recreation, craftwork and conversation, and to make new friends. The clubs meet in four different locations in the county and would be unable to function without our ambulance which was provided with the assistance of Help the Aged. An important part of our programme is our 'Lunch Box' which serves 200 meals every week, thus providing nourishment for those who might otherwise be unable to prepare it.

THE BARNABAS TRUST
Enniskillen Methodist Church
Darling Street
Enniskillen
Co Fermanagh

Tel: (0365) 325318

CO-LECK CARE

Who are we?

Co   – Co-Operation
Leck   – Leckpatrick
Care   – Caring

When were we formed?

We were formed in January 1988

Why were we formed?

Following the tragic death, in November 1987, of a local lady and her young grand-daughter in a road accident near their home, the congregation of the local Presbyterian church, to which the lady belonged, proposed to their minister that they should hold a collection for the bereaved family. The Minister, after much deliberation, consulted his local Church of Ireland counterpart and they decided to call a public meeting to discuss what could be done.

Before the meeting began the local Roman Catholic Parish Priest arrived with several members of his congregation. It was decided to hold another meeting which was announced in all three churches. This meeting duly took place and was well attended by all denominations. It was decided that instead of the money being given to the family concerned it should be put to a use which would benefit the whole community.

From this Co-Leck was born.

What have we achieved?

In March of that year a door-to-door collection of every house in the Leckpatrick Parish area was held. Teams of three, one from each of the Churches, visited each home. The sum of approximately £8700 was raised and used to buy a portable ventilator and accessories for use in the intensive care unit of Altnagelvin Hospital.

In 1989 the collection was again held and the sum of £6500 was raised and presented to the management team of the new Foyle Hospice. This money will be used to furnish a room for the use of families of terminally ill cancer patients and will be known as the Co-Leck Care Room.

This year the collectors raised a total of £5000, of which £250 was used to purchase a monitor to check the heartbeat of unborn babies. This is now in the safe hands of our community midwives.

The balance of this year's collection was used to equip a suite of rooms in the local health centre. This is to provide our doctors with the facilities needed to carry out minor operations requiring local anaesthetic.

What we hope to achieve

Currently we are looking into the possibility of providing employment through the ACE scheme for local people who will help the elderly, needy and handicapped in our area with a variety of household jobs and repairs. We hope to have this scheme in full operation by the end of the year.

Cross Community relations are the most important part of our organisation and we hope to keep these alive and through our efforts make our area one of peace and harmony.

The collections from which Co-Leck Care grew will continue for as long as people support us and while there are local causes worthy of our support.

CO-LECK CARE
15 Lowertown Road
Ballymagorry
Strabane
Co Tyrone
BT82 OLE

Tel (0504) 883483

NEW MOSSLEY COUNCIL OF CHURCHES

1. History

In October 1983 a meeting of many of the clergy from the Newtownabbey area took place in Elmfield House, Glengormley. There was a very good response from the clergy and many churches were represented. The meeting was very successful and included some very good discussion and prayer. It was generally agreed that such a meeting was both good and beneficial.

Unfortunately because of the large number involved it was difficult, if not impossible, to assemble such a gathering with any great degree of success. However, a small group of ministers who worked in the New Mossley area of Newtownabbey felt that it would be a great tragedy if such an opportunity to meet again was not grasped. They felt that because of their small number and their common concern they should be able to at least meet, if not work, together. So, early in December 1983, the first meeting of the New Mossley Council of Churches took place. At that stage it was just an informal meeting of four ministers - Rev Hugh Hopkins, Church of the Holy Spirit (Church of Ireland), Rev Dereck Haskins, Mossley Methodist Church, Rev William Harshaw, New Mossely Presbyterian Church and Rev Sean Emerson, St MacNissi's Church (Roman Catholic). No one realised that the group would grow and become formal.

Over the next few months there was much discussion and gradually a sense of trust developed between the ministers. Just about the time that the ministers were getting to know each other better there arose an opportunity to develop a cross-community holiday scheme sponsored by the Hall Green Council of Churches in Birmingham. This involved sending thirty children, fifteen Protestant and fifteen Roman Catholic, for a ten-day holiday in Birmingham. Meanwhile the Council of Churches was developing and growing, mainly among the four clergy at this stage. There was much honest discussion and so it was eventually agreed that, while there were important theological differences between our traditions, we all believed in the Gospel of Christ - the Gospel which calls on all to love their neighbour.

The ministers felt that they shared many concerns about the development of New Mossley and determined on a concerted effort in tackling these concerns. Many of the issues that caused such trouble in the wider community were to be found in New Mossley - social issues such as high unemployment, the pressures on the family, lack of facilities on the estate and the lack of dignity afforded to the community - these and many more were present and the clergy were at pains to let it be known that they cared for every person in the community, not just the members of their respective churches. These concerns and problems needed to be tackled and because they were a common worry than a united response was very important. They were all too aware that this was an opportunity, a golden opportunity, for Roman Catholic and Protestants to live and work in harmony.

The group of clergy continued to discuss and address the problems facing them and affecting the estate. It was not all plain sailing and not always straightforward progress. However, the holiday project continued, a Carol Service was held each Christmas, such as the Youth Club Project and a newsletter, published and distributed to each family in the estate on a few occasions. Problems often arose because of the changing political issues and personnel moves among the clergy. However, if there was to be an effective witness to the Gospel then all such problems had to be resolved. On that basis of mutual trust and respect the group continued to grow and develop, a growth which is not yet finished.

2. Leadership

On occasions it was necessary to speak out boldy and fearlessly where it was evident that issues of such moment were facing the community that only be declaring unequivocally where they, as ministers of the Gospel of Christ, stood would tense situations be avoided and communal peace and harmony be maintained. One such occasion was shortly after the signing of the Anglo-Irish Agreement when some families were being attacked. A letter signed by the four ministers was delivered to every household and read as follows:

'As the clergy of the four main churches working in New

Mossley, we wish to pass on to you our guidance and teaching in the present difficult situation in the country, and in particular as it affects our estate. We wish to condemn and stand against the cowardly and evil intimidation and thuggery which a minority has recently engaged in. Already some families have been intimidated and at least one family has been driven from the estate. Putting anyone from their home, or frightening and threatening them in it, is a particularly low and nasty crime. If those who carry out the attacks think for one moment that they do so in the name of their religion then let them hear loud and clear, in our name, and in the name of Jesus Christ, that their actions, which are wicked, sinful cowardly and mindless, are unacceptable to true Christianity. This statement is made from the standpoint of the Christian faith and of all that is right and decent. We want to provide a lead on behalf of the people of New Mossley in the stand against this evil. We encourage you all to stand united against these things before it is too late and their dirty work has spread too far. Disown these people and their actions. Attempt to spread love and understanding within the estate. If you know of anyone who is facing intimidation, or if you are, then please get in touch with us as individuals or a group and we will try to do what we can'.

This letter had the desired effect of reassuring the people of estate as had a second letter distributed the following July when there were fears of communal unrest. The response to these initiatives showed that the Council of Churches was accepted and their leadership appreciated. The Council hopes to continue to provide credible leadership.

3. Developments

Mention has already been made of one of the earliest developments in the life of the Council of Churches - the Birmingham Holiday Project. Since 1984 30 children - 15 Roman Catholic and 5 from each of the three Protestant Churches, have been able to holiday together through the kindness of the Hall Green Council of Churches in Birmingham. Each church appoints a leader and although each leader represents a denomination, as far as the children are concerned the leadership is on a joint basis.

Children going on the holiday must be between the ages of 12 and 14, an age group which is old enough to understand the aspirations of the Project and young enough to see that 'different' doesn't necessarily mean 'bad'. The parents of the children attend at least one preparatory meeting prior to the trip so that they can be fully informed of the aims of the programme, the travel arrangements and the rules to which the children will have to adhere. A number of meetings are held for the children before the trip so that they can get to know one another and meet the leaders who will be travelling with them. On reaching their destination the children are placed with host families, usually of a different denomination. The children meet for joint activities each day. The Sunday is devoted to Church-going with the children encouraged to attend serviced in churches not of their own denomination and culminating in a Joint Service which is held in a different church each year.

When they return home the lay committee organises a reunion weekend at which the emphasis is on enjoying themselves but with a Joint Service on the Sunday to remind them that there is a more serious side to the proceedings.

We are in the process of trying to contact all the young people who have taken part in the programme over the past 6 years with a view to bringing them back together again to build on what was begun in Birmingham. We are trying to help them see that, while they may differ from each other in denomination, there is a lot which binds them together, so that no matter what they may see or hear to the contrary, they will know that it is possible for Roman Catholics and Protestants to live and pray together without fear.

Inside the past twelve months two new and exciting developments have occurred which will provide further opportunities for part-nership at a very influential level.

The first is the prospect of developing a community centre in the estate. This has been greatly aided by the willingness of the Housing Executive, to provide an unused building for development as a 'heart' for an estate which is bereft of any facilities. Funding is actively being sought and it is hoped to start work within the next few months on the provision of premises where people can meet and which do not carry a denominational tag.

The second development is the transfer of the existing ACE scheme to the sponsorship of the Council of Churches. Until November of last year Mossely Community Project was an ACE Scheme sponsored by the Mossley Methodist Church. As a token of their belief that the Scheme should be seen to be for the benefit of the whole community the Methodist Church, after discussion with the Department of Economic Development, invited the Council of Churches to become the sponsoring body. The Scheme is managed by a Committee which is gradually becoming interdenominational with representatives from each of the participating churches.

The Council of Churches itself has moved away from being made up solely of ministers. There are now two lay representatives of each church on the Executive Committee and they share fully in leadership as well as the work being undertaken.

Together these developments provide an excellent opportunity to promote unity in our community, unity based on mutual respect. The New Mossley Council of Churches has survived and developed over the last seven years despite changes in personnel. It has continually encouraged members of the various churches to work together through an on-going process of education and example. In a very socially deprived area the New Mossely Council of Churches is a beacon of hope for all and especially for the people of New Mossley. In the face of apathy, need and insularity, New Mossley has the potential in some small way, under God, to point the way forward to hope for our country, encouragement for our people and a spirit of openness between our different traditions.

NEW MOSSLEY COUNCIL OF CHURCHES
3 Swanstown Drive
Newtownabbey
Co Antrim
BT36 8DP

Tel: (0232) 840308 (office)

Rev. Tom Craig:

I would like to lead the Conference in a warm and heart-felt salute, not only to the speakers but also to the projects and the people they represent. They are people who see themselves as ordinary but they are doing things that some of us think extraordinary.

PART IV

SUMMARY OF CONFERENCE DISCUSSIONS

DISCUSSION

EDITORIAL NOTE

In the afternoon, the 170 conference delegates divided into five discussion groups before reporting back to a plenary session and concluding proceedings with an open forum. At the time, there was no intention to publish the conference proceedings, so there was no tape-recording nor shorthand transcript. But each of the groups wprked towards answering some specific questions and noted comments towards that goal. Three of the five discussion groups have offered brief summaries of the thrust of their dialogues. Two are recorded in the form of quotations. In each case, we preface them with the questions CCCCW asked them to answer, which in turn other groups may wish to consider. We offer them as examples of the kinds of comments Christians make in inter-Church discussion. If you are reading this as part of a study group, you may find echoes of what you yourselves have to say. We begin with the questions:

REPORT FROM DISCUSSION GROUP ON THE TROUBLES AND ITS VICTIMS

Leader

The Rev Sam Burch seconded to the Cornerstone Community

Questions:

1. What experience do members of the group have in assisting 'victims' of the 'Troubles'?
2. What are their special needs? Are they in any way different from other bereaved people?
3. What can we offer them?
4. How do we help local congregations and communities deal with the aftermath of a terrorist act? What sort of negative feelings might be expected?
5. Is there any form of back-up, or preparation that might be offered to pastors and people?
6. Are there any initiatives that members of the group might wish to take in their own areas?

Report (in the form of unattributed quotations from members of the discussion group)

1. 'There is a difference between ordinary bereavement and bereavement which has been caused by a violent act'.

2. 'It is necessary at some stage to talk with the victim about the question of forgiveness of those responsible for the violent death, but one needs to be sensitive about the time at which the matter is broached'.

3. 'The way the media demand instant statements is an invasion of personal privacy. In my area there have been 27 troubles related assassinations. In such an environment the Gospel comes alive.

But the perceptions of the Gospels which each church has are not big enough to help us face up to the situation. We need to open ourselves to what our sister churches are saying and to learn from each other'.

4. 'After the nun was killed in the bomb in Co. Armagh her colleagues were advised to prepare a statement for the media and just to read it to them. This proved very satisfactory'.

5. 'The family and friends of a victim may find it helpful to appoint a spokesperson to deal with the media. The media will often understand and accept this, and it takes pressure off the victim'.

6. 'Much thought needs to be given to what the person conducting the funeral service should say. In many cases overtly political matters are brought in, and the effect can be very painful for the victim'.

7. 'Coming up to the first anniversary of the Enniskillen bombing, a social worker talked to relatives about how they might cope with media attention, and this proved helpful'.

8. 'There can be a danger in over-protecting a victim or the bereaved. They have to be helped to face life'.

9. 'There are more victims than just the bereaved'.

10. 'Paramilitaries are also victims, and also part of us. Our forgiveness must stretch to them'.

11. 'We are in danger of blurring the distinction between right and wrong'.

12. 'The distinction between sin and the sinner is helpful'.

13. 'We should not judge other people's reactions about forgiveness'.

14. 'Is it possible to have forgiveness where there is no repentance?'

15. 'We should not always think of anger as wrong'.

16. 'Overstatement of bitterness is helpful. Too glib forgiveness is unhelpful'.

17. 'Righteousness indignation has a place. Forgiveness is preventing our reaction from doing damage inside ourselves'.

18. 'It is important not to be partisan in our grief'.

19. 'Church leaders have found difficulty in projecting cross-community forgiveness'.

20. 'We need to talk, Protestant and Catholics, how we feel about events'.

21. 'We have been talking like this for over 15 years'.

22. 'In the Springfield Road, the so-called Catholic Reaction Group, in retaliation for sectarian shootings by Protestants wanted to get rid of the few Protestant families in the area. The Methodists invited local Catholics to come to functions in their church. The Methodists also went to the house of the bereaved widow of a sectarian murder by Protestants, and were warmly welcomed. So far none of the remaining Protestant families have felt they had to leave'.

23. 'The question which I take away in my mind is how can we extend discussions of this type to the many many churches where they are no part of ordinary church life?'

REPORT FROM DISCUSSION GROUP ON THE CHURCHES AND LOCAL COMMUNITY NEEDS

Leader

The Rev Raymond Fox, C of I, Carryduff

Questions:

1. What kinds of local needs has the experience of members of the group made them aware of?
2. What part has the local church to play in seeking to meet those local needs?
3. How does the work of the churches fit in with the work of statutory bodies?
4. Is there any advantage in trying to work inter-church? Do the churches by their deferences make it more difficult to deal with community problems?
5. What can local church groups do? Where can they get help? What kind of help can they get?
6. What initiatives do members of the group think they might take in their own areas?

Report (again, a selection of unattributed quotations to convey the flavour of the group"s discussion)

1. 'Churches can initiate projects to enable neglected towns to get government recognition and grants'.

2. 'Churches can do this through launching a local community newspaper'.

3. 'Or they can petition publications that give bad publicity'.

4. 'Just uniting at times of tension and tragedy can help'.

5. 'But the churches must be careful - when is it the time to come

out as visible partners? Will the publicity generated be counter-productive?'

6. 'Perhaps publicity-seeking ventures are not the way forward. Much more is achieved if there is ongoing private cross-community communication - activities which never make the headlines, hospital collections, work among the homeless, etc. In a situation where misrepresentation and myths abound we should not worry if no one hears about what is happening - so long as it is being done'.

7. 'But publicity can help challenge the myths and inspire others'.

8. 'Churches must not duplicate other work or try to create a role for themselves artificially. Their task should be to initiate what needs to be done where there is a gap in the social service'.

9. 'The churches should support what good work is already being done by better qualified people than the clergy'.

10. 'We should encourage members to active involvement in fields of service where their gifts are needed'.

11. 'We need to protect our members from an isolation or "apartheid", eg. *Church* Bowling Club, *Church* Mens' Groups, *Church* Women's Groups, instead of encouraging integration into the community'.

12. 'If the Churches realise their role as servants of the community they will prevent an over-dependence on "Church-based" organisation'.

13. 'But there is a need for leadership - especially if there is ever to be joint-worship'.

14. 'A Castlederg-based group has no official clergy membership, but has been active in meeting local community needs, while still being "inter-Church"'.

15. 'For an initiative to be particularly effective, not only is leadership necessary but also a "mandate", ie. a substantial proportion

of the people in the pew to give active support to a project. There needs to be a degree of "grass roots" movement'.

16. 'Even statutory bodies will only function effectively when they are in touch with the needs of the people, perhaps as identified by various Church groups. Their role is essentially supportive. In the Shankill Road area a statutory body was sufficiently confident in the work of the Churches that it made the initial approach, asking the Churches to nominate members for a Committee to oversee a joint distribution of finances'.

17. 'The statutory bodies also have a role in working in areas where the young people are "unchurched" and bringing these areas to the knowledge and attention of the Churches'.

18. 'Although no one wishes to lose their identity, identity does not primarily lie in a youth club or badminton team - these are two examples where unity could be brought about where currently there are two or three separate clubs in one small town'.

19. 'The churches can best help be emphasising *individual* inter-action, leaving the inter-relation between structures to those whose vocation it is to work in that area'.

20. 'Although there are exceptions, leadership by example is often necessary from priests and ministers before their congregation members will be motivated'.

21. 'At the heart of our troubles is mistrust and prejudices between communities. Therefore, if crises arise which threaten to divide us further, there must be an example given by the Churches in inter-church statements and action'.

REPORT FROM DISCUSSION GROUP ON THE CHURCHES AND FAITH

Leader

Rev Gerry Reynolds, Redemptorist, Clonard, and Cornerstone.

Questions:

1. Where and how does our Faith become relevant to community relations and inter-church community action? For example, through the Spirit of Christ in us, or through obedience to His commands, or through the inevitable effect of being converted?
2. Do the differences in teaching between the Churches present hindrances to our working together? If there are such hindrances what are they? How important are they? Is the temptation to exaggerate them or to minimise them?
3. What effect do cultural, social and political issues have on the deferences in faith?
4. What common basis can we find to share, in our inter-discipleship of Jesus Christ?
5. Faith is not only belief, it is also Trust. What relevance does our trust in God have for us, in our situation here?
6. Are there any initiatives that members of the group feel they want to take in their own locality with the other churches?

Report:

1. Our group started looking at faith as freedom from fear. Do not be afraid. We moved on from that to looking at faith as right belief, the way in which we are made right with God. Then to seeing faith as being living witnesses to our God whose love is infinite, whose Son died on the Cross for all. Faith in that sense of being pilgrims together on the road to Jericho caring for all in need, in a right relationship with one another at a personal and institutional level.

2. One of the group said there was a youth group of ages 17-22 in his parish in West Belfast which has been trying to find a youth group of another church that they could meet. That problem was solved. How wonderful it would be if the CCCCW could help match other groups who were reaching out to their fellow churches.

3. Then one of the group spoke about feeling bereft in his new Parish because for the first time in his life as a clergyman he doesn't have any clergy fraternal. He was encouraged to take some initiative in his own area.

4. Another Minister spoke about visiting the Catholic Parish Priest of his area but not doing it without the approval and backing of the Elders of his congregation.

5. Two other people spoke about the question of developing church media. One spoke about the new PACE magazine which Alf McCreary will edit. CCCCW might take an initiative to help the PACE magazine or launch its own newsletter/magazine to focus more on community work.

6. We must pray together to deepen our faith. We must work harder together as an expression of our faith.

REPORT FROM DISCUSSION GROUP ON THE CHURCHES AND THE UNEMPLOYED

Leader

The Rev David Chillingworth, C of I, Seagoe,
Portadown. Killicomaine Care Project

Questions:

1. What experience have the members of the group had of this problem?
2. Is this the Churches' business? If it is, why?
3. How does the Churches' role here relate to the statutory services?
4. Where can we get help to support this kind of work?
5. What can be done by local churches to help the unemployed?
6. What initiatives might members of the group have decided upon for their own locality?

Report:

1. All the members of the group agreed that unemployment, for whatever reason is a soul-destroying experience, and that the church as a body, and we, as simply individuals had a moral responsibility to reach out and help, in whatever way possible, to those who find themselves in such situations.

2. The group shared experiences of where they saw unemployment had an effect, not only on individuals, but on that person's whole family - breakdown of marriages, family units, alcohol abuse, violence, to some extent the group felt unemployment could be the cause of such problems. Many members pointed to the fact that areas with a high level of unemployment, also suffered high levels of violence or petty crime.

3. All agreed that the experience of long term unemployment was
    degrading - people saw themselves as being of little use or value.
    They lost dignity and sometimes even lost hope.

4. The value of schemes such as 'ACE' was discussed in much
    depth. Most agreed that ACE played an important role in
    helping long term unemployed to discover once again what a
    worthwhile person they are.

    The 52 weeks helped them to regain lost confidence and self
    esteem, and in some instances even if they did not find permanent
    employment, individuals were showing leadership in their com-
    munities in a voluntary capacity which is most worthwhile.

5. Members agreed that while 'ACE' is money well spent, the
    uncertainty of how long this would last was a very worrying
    aspect. Most delegates felt that after another 3 years, 'ACE'
    would no longer exist. Most expressed concern about how not
    only the unemployed would suffer, but how communities would
    suffer if this were to happen. To this end, the delegates felt that
    the churches should be looking at assisting the unemployed
    through church-based initiatives, such as enterprise training
    units, job clubs, job search support groups, clinics and so forth.
    Some churches have already started implementing plans for the
    future. One clergyman has over the past year collected enough
    money from his local community to enable him to form a
    limited company. They are now producing various articles
    which are made in craft workshops, these are sold to the public
    and income is generated into the company.

6. The churches have buildings, halls, etc., that could/should be
    used to promote such developments. Furthermore, within
    congregations there is a wealth of untapped talent that should
    be appealed to, so as to assist with such initiatives. Many
    professional people could further witness to their Christianity
    by being involved in such things as advice clinics, etc. Ministers,
    Priests and Clergy in general, should speak in public and call for
    this witness.

REPORT FROM DISCUSSION GROUP
ON DEALING WITH ADDICTION

Leader

Rev Derrick Haskins, Methodist, Bangor, formerly
Whitewell Community Group, formerly Barnabas

Questions:

1. What experience have members of the group had of dealing
   with people who have an addiction problem?
2. What understanding do members of the group have of people
   who become hooked? What leads to addiction
3. What can we offer to the community to deal with addiction?
   Health education, campaigns against new licences, alternatives
   to alcohol, rehabilitation?
4. Are there any advantages in working on an inter-church basis?
   Are there any disadvantages? Are there marked differences of
   attitude between the churches on this issue?
5. Can we, should we, avoid being moralistic about addiction?
   What are our motives for taking an interest in this issue?
6. Are there any initiatives that members of the group have
   decided on as a result of their discussions?

Report:

1. The group recognised that the problem of addiction is a very
   wide one, including drugs, solvent abuse, gambling, addiction
   to vital medicines and even stealing fast cars. However we
   discussed these along the lines of alcoholism - the form of
   addiction with which we were most familiar in dealing. A group
   of people shared their insights gained from visiting an addiction centre in the United States. They particularly pointed out
   that addiction is a disease in the recognised medical sense, and
   so requires both medical and 'social' help, ie. counselling and

community support. The centre they visited boasted a 35% success rate, compared to a 15% success rate published by some local initiatives.

2.   The group felt that the root cause of any predisposition to addiction being activated was hopelessness and the church is alone able to offer hope, and yet the church has no pat answers. When it comes to treating the addict you cannot say 'Be saved, and all will be well'. There are no easy answers to complex issues. Addiction is a physical, a psychological and a spiritual problem, the clergy can only deal with the third.

3.   We recognised that it is not just the addict who suffers, but also his work and his family. Very often the family are used to point out someone's addiction problem. It was felt that inviting spouses and parents to an open meeting was not helpful, as this labelled families in distress. Trained counsellors therefore were needed in order to help the root problem.

4.   It was pointed out that the last people the addict would turn to was the clergy, as traditionally they are seen as 'moralisers' - condemning those who over-step the moral mark. Rather we should not condemn, taking the example of Jesus with the woman caught in adultery, 'I do not condemn you, go your way and sin no more'. The church should aim for education to the dangers of drink and drugs. It was pointed out again and again that there is no place for morality in chemical addiction. So we must not point the finger of blame.

5.   The group discussed the problem of heavy teenage drinking. One person noticed parents leaving their teenage children at licensed premises, and wondered at the police and community's inability to cope with this.

6.   There is also the problem of gaming machines among the young. The sort of machine that seems to promise that you would win the next time. There are examples of people being addicted to the flashing lights. One person wanted these machines banned totally.

7.   Should the churches work together to oppose, for example, the

planning of pubs near churches and youth clubs? Sometimes churches have been successful in closing such premises. It was pointed out, however, that this does not solve the problem. As in Prohibition days, drinking is simply driven underground. Once again the place of education was stressed - to encourage people to drink sensibly.

8. So what is being done? A centre working with alcoholics in Omagh was much praised. This centre gives a very severe six week course, aiming to reform alcoholics in particular. It invites members of the families to visit at weekends, when they are counselled about the disease. Among other positive initiatives that were discussed were pubs with no beer, and alcohol free drinks - creating a friendly, social atmosphere where people can relax without the need to drink. Although the demise of the Roman Catholic 'pioneer' scheme was noted, there was much praise for the new 'one day at a time' scheme recently launched by the main churches in Armagh. These are examples of the good work being done by the churches together. Addiction affects all communities. There is absolutely no reason for any 'apartheid' in responding. We hope for more resources to provide positive professional treatment. We must commit ourselves to be more able to care on a personal level. We, the churches, must offer hope.

PART V

CONCLUSION

OPEN FORUM

Perhaps exhausted by their discussion groups, the delegates were reluctant to speak in their 'open forum'. So the chairman of the session offered to provoke debate by asking questions. By now the CCCCW was beginning to think that the proceedings should be recorded, so there is a verbatim transcript of this session:

1. Simon Lee

'Is there a distinct role for the Churches in what you might call "Social Work" that is distinct from say the Government's role? Is there a specifically religious mission in this work?'

Barney Filer, Church of Ireland Board for Social Responsibility
    'Apart from the ACE scheme, a valuable scheme no doubt but of very limited value in solving the underlying unemployment problem, there are other schemes which are trying to tackle *long-term* unemployment. Schemes both for training and for providing places of employment. I have in mind the YTP network which provides two years' training leading to City and Guilds or other qualifications and in very many cases to permanent work. I have in mind the Enterprise parts which offer start-up work space at a favourable rate, administrative support, marketing skills and so on. All of these schemes, and there are very many of them, are run by voluntary boards and management on which many Churchmen are represented. I see quite a number here today and I feel that these schemes and others of that sort offer much better hope of long-term employment than the ACE scheme.'

Grace Bennett
    'The Churches should indeed be making moves now to fill the gap that is going to be left by ACE. Our group made some suggestions about what Ministers or Priests could do with their congregations

now to create initiatives that would help and perhaps bring the community round. Then they would be ready to take over if ACE is withdrawn - that gap would be filled.'

2. Simon Lee

'Is there a role for joint Church statements?'

Father Reynolds

'Just to mention a particular issue - the four UDR men in Armagh are in prison for about six years and it looks to my analysis of it very like the Guildford Four. These are very difficult ones to handle and I remember when we were asking for support for a petition for the Guildford Four and Birmingham Six quite a number of clergy said they would have nothing to do with it because they didn't want to be involved in politics. What is the prophetic role of the Church in situations like that? Can we exercise a ministry together when institutions seem to have failed to do the things that they were instituted to do?'

David Montgomery, Lucan Youth Centre

'I am quite heartened to hear Father Reynolds make mention of that because it is the first time I have heard someone from the Roman Catholic community mention the UDR Four. I think I have yet to hear a public statement by a member of the Protestant clergy mentioning the Birmingham Six. I think this has been going on for too long and if people are informed about these things - it took me a while to be informed about the exact details of the case - but once they are, surely they should not be divided along traditional loyalties?'

3. Simon Lee

'Could I raise a point where I think that I perhaps had the wrong emphasis this morning? When I was talking about fear of the other I don't want us to forget that it is often a question of fear of our "own". In reaching out to others from a different community background or denomination - it isn't just fear of them because they'll probably be very friendly - it's fear of people behind your shoulder who are going to look askance at your initiatives. Any views - is this a problem and can anything be done?'

Canon Jim Sides, Florencecourt, Enniskillen

'I think in a way we are all far too nice today, so much goodness and kindness and understanding, all agreeing - there's no kind of hate. You go back to the communities - the problem is there. I come from Florencecourt, seven miles beyond Enniskillen where people have been very deeply affected by the things what have happened there - people murdered or badly injured in the community. One of the problems I did outline in our discussion group - we have developed cross-community groups, one on history and one supporting medical practice but that is done in spite of the problem of peoples' suspicions. We are a funny kind of community in a way. If someone's cow is ill they go to and help the neighbour but if it was something else if it was a neighbour whose son was IRA, it might be a different. This seems rather strange but what do you do about people say who are information carriers - if I had Roman Catholic scouts in my scout group, others would be afraid of information being carried. Whenever someone is shot or blown up in the community it's alleged that local people in the Roman Catholic community set it up and it's very hard to answer that one because I wouldn't like to be responsible for anyone's death in the sense of someone being betrayed or set up. The same as the Orangemen in our community who go to an Orange Lodge meeting and trip off to the Half-way Inn or somewhere and are sitting round talking at a table about what people are doing in the community and they don't know who is listening. There is a real problem of fear of information being carried.'

John Doherty

'My own experience is that I have come into the town where I lived twelve years ago and four years ago I sent my children to an 80% Protestant school. I'm a Catholic. Now I have been speaking to people at other times who say "Yes - its easy for you - you're seen as cross-community". The thing about being seen as cross-community means that you have to stand up and be counted which I am prepared to do and prepared to let history be my judge. Unfortunately when you grow up in an area particularly if it is an area which is 80% one or 80% the other and people are looking over their shoulder - they don't do what they feel in their heart -they do what they think the neighbours will either let them do or not criticise them for and I think this is where we have to stand up and be counted to do what we believe is right. I would like to congratulate this Conference today - I think five years ago this Conference couldn't have been held and I would like to say that I have not heard one negative word today.'

Rev Stephen Crowther, St Christopher's, Belfast
  'One big difference between North and South is what was mentioned by the last speaker - suspicion. Somehow Northern Ireland has got to overcome its chronic suspicion and doubt. It's almost an inability on some people's part to see that there can be good and genuine intentions on the part of people they don't know. I find it a constant problem even talking to people - not only in cross-community relationships but even within different groups within your "own" community. I don't know specifically what the way forward is but I think as Churches that is one of the central cores of the culture here that we really have to deal with - people's chronic suspicion because people can't reach out even in their own communities when that suspicion is there.'

4. Simon Lee

'I wonder if anyone has got any constructive thoughts about the role of the media in all this work? Do the groups we heard from this morning really want more publicity? Do they want the good news to come out through the media or would that in some way compromise what is being done? Do you think people in Northern Ireland realise the work that is going on? Do the media cover this too much or not enough?'

Sam Burch, Cornerstone
  'It's a very very sensitive area, the area we are in, we took a decision not to have media coverage. The media were most understanding and sympathetic and said if you want publicity lift the phone and we will be glad to give you coverage. We have let it come out in a natural way whenever people ask for articles in magazines and so on we have done that now and again we have been dragged into publicity. Part of the problem is that the suspicions mean that if you are portrayed in the media there's a spate of abusive phone calls, disruptive phone calls, sometimes hate letters which are mostly from nut-cases but they can be very hurtful and difficult to deal with. Also you bring a lot of criticism even from people of your own community like the Churches will misunderstand what you are trying to do so it's

understandable that most of us try to keep a low profile but having said that I do understand the need for a wider constituency to understand the positives that are going on'.

5. Simon Lee

'Could I ask any overseas visitor for reflections on our discussions?'

Professor McAllister

'I am struck with a couple of things - words that are used by everyone which each person assumes to mean the same thing - it seems to me actually mean some things quite different. For example when people use the phrase "the people of God" I wonder exactly what it is that is inside peoples' heads when they use that phrase if some of us on the globe are the people of God who are the rest of us? I think also of the United States which has large proportions of Jews, Muslims, Buddists, as well as Christians - how are they thought of in the context of the kind of discussion which is going on here today. I also wonder about the distinction between the word "the Church" and "the Churches". I wonder what is in people's heads when they use a word like "the Church". Then we say the Church is the people of God but exactly who are the people who make up the Church and what is the distinction between the Church and Churches. I am listening very much as an outsider trying to understand what people in Northern Ireland are thinking about when they are using very common, very everyday terms that one wouldn't ordinarily ask about'.

6. Simon Lee

'Would anyone like to offer final comments on any of these matters?'

David McKittrick, Protestant and Catholic Encounter:

'I would like to say four things: One in answer to Father Reynold's question to the Churches about the question of miscarriages of justice. I think that the Churches do take on board the monitoring of progress of miscarriages of justice. "Living the Kingdom" for instance, the book which has been produced by the Faith and Justice Group. The Presbyterian Assembly has a Committee which reported this year which I attended on the particular day when they were dealing with politics and the Churches' role in politics. I know that here is a Committee which has been appointed by the Assembly which does in fact monitor all of these cases which are in dispute.

The second thing I would like to say is about fear that Simon Lee mentioned of your own looking over your shoulder and knowing that they know what's going on and about a friend here who mentioned the problems of Ministers who may be working in Parishes where talk can be dangerous. In some PACE groups people travel from quite a distance out of their own area and come to a PACE group in another area to avoid that problem so that there they can speak freely and I was a little bit disturbed at the very beginning of the day when it was said we're not just another talk shop. I would just like to make a plug for talk. Talk is not cheap - talk can be very powerful, telling your story if you're a Catholic talking to a Protestant, or vice-versa can be a very powerful statement especially if it's listened to. So talk *is* doing something. Talk *is* powerful. People have often criticised PACE groups because they talk but talking is wonderful. If you can get Catholics and Protestants together to talk about things that divide us, my goodness, isn't that wonderful! Let's have *more* talking shops.

The third thing I want to say about the media is that PACE does two things about the media - we use them when we need them. For instance, when we're having a Conference, we have found the media to be very helpful. But if we're getting politicians together we want them to talk freely and wouldn't want the press there. In this case the press would come at the beginning of discussions and then leave. This is very helpful.

The last thing is a thank you for organising the day and allowing us to have this public expression of the fact that the Churches are interested in becoming public in networking and in getting people to communicate with each other.'

7. Simon Lee

'In such a big group it is difficult for everybody to contribute by saying something. The questions are: what are we going to say *next* and *where* are we going to say it? What are we going to *do* next and where are we going to *do* it? The Churches' Central Committee would welcome ideas on future initiatives, whether you want more local Conferences or other big Conferences like this, or whether you think a Conference specifically for, say, young people ought to be the next step. They would also like to know if you feel that there will be any value in the Conference proceedings being made more widely available, perhaps in a book form and relatively quickly at that. ("Yes" came the reply from various parts of the hall - hence this volume). The CCCCW would be grateful for ideas on other initiatives. In a moment, I will ask the CCCCW Chairman to conclude our day. May I just thank you for allowing me to be a part of this literally hope-ful experience? May I say that one message is clearly going out to all Christians in Northern Ireland from Cookstown today and that is a call to action.'

Rev Tom Craig
    'I would now like to close proceedings by leading the Conference in worship. As St Paul wrote to the Romans, Chapter 12 verses 1 & 2 (Good News Bible translation):-

"So then, my brothers, because of God's great mercy to us I appeal to you: Offer yourselves as a living sacrifice to God, dedicated to his service and pleasing to him. This is the true worship that you should offer. Do not conform yourselves to the standards of this world, but let God transform you inwardly by a complete change of your mind. Then you will be able to know the will of God – what is good and pleasing to him and is perfect."

Let us say together, "The grace of the Lord Jesus Christ, the love of God, and the fellowship of the Holy Spirit be with you all, now and ever more. Amen." '

CALL TO ACTION

(A personal view from Simon Lee)

Immediately after the conference, I was asked to specify what I meant by my concluding remarks. What action? By whom?

What follows is my personal summary of the spirit of the conference. Others present may have discerned different wishes. Readers should treat this call to action as a personal observation but one I hope, worth reflecting on as at least influenced by this moving day. The call is directed to lay Christians in Northern Ireland, to their church leaders, to the government, to businessmen and to all people of goodwill inside and outside Northern Ireland:

1. TALKING TOGETHER

Church leaders must be seen to be talking, praying and working together. Contrary to those who sneer at 'talking shops', talk *is* action. The CCCCW must organise local, regional, specific topic (eg. employment), and specific audience (eg. youth) conferences to follow up this meeting. Local inter-church groups must be encouraged to meet together and the resources and expertise of the Community Relations Council should be brought to help such groups.

2. MEDIA TOGETHER

The churches must publicise the Good News of reconciliation. There must be a properly funded, professionally produced inter-church magazine. Contacts with the secular media must continue to be developed since local groups are given enormous confidence when they see how others have negotiated the path of reconciliation. Inter-church groups should come to terms not only with the press but also with television and radio. There is enormous potential for good work through these media. The BBC in Northern Ireland and Ulster Television are to be congratulated on their contributions to charity (particularly Children in Need and the ITV Telethon respectively). The people of Northern Ireland have a reputation for great generosity on these occasions. Perhaps inter-church groups could work together on local projects for these great days and thus also contribute to reconciliation.

3. EDUCATION TOGETHER

The four main churches have now agreed a common curriculum for Religious Education. I applaud their achievement and the efforts of schools, churches and government in developing wonderful educational programmes in Education for Mutual Understanding and Cultural Heritage. No doubt, the CCCCW's Schools' History Project had, and has, a part to play in all this. But I would call for further action on at least two fronts:

(a) Parents are understandably bewildered but excited by such developments as EMU and Cultural Heritage. I would like the four churches and others to come together locally throughout Northern Ireland to provide joint courses for parents in these matters. To that end I append the relevant documents to this book. Such courses would have enormous benefit not merely in enabling parents to support their children but also to meet together and begin to understand one another better.

(b) I would also like to ask all the churches to look again at their attitude to integrated education. These schools regularly con-tain a clause in their Memorandum and Articles of Association and other foundation documents, which stresses the Christian, not secular, nature of the education they endeavour to provide. Have we, as churches, done enough to help these new schools flourish in that worthy aim?

4. FAMILIES TOGETHER

All the churches talk about family life but more could be done to support the family. Northern Ireland has its share of single parent families, particularly teenage mothers, who are sometimes crying out for help from their relatives and communities. Northern Ireland has more than its share of child abuse of all types. The time has long since come for greater education in family life, especially the responsibilities of sexuality and parenthood. A helpline for parents, let alone for children, is urgently needed. Funding must be found. Local facilities must be made available for 'drop-in' centres, so that the loneliness of the single parent can be countered. The churches must overcome any attitude of disdain for the teenage mother. Those who hate the sin must still love the sinners and must certainly act to help their children.

5. CARING TOGETHER

A major problem for all communities here is addiction:

  to alcohol
  to violence
  to gambling
  to drugs
  to 'joy-riding'.

The churches should not exaggerate the problems (eg. gambling) and should not pretend that there is a spiritual answer to a medical problem (eg alcoholism), nor should they continue to put off addicts by moralising. What they should do is quite simple:

  (a) offer practical help, utilising their resources

  (b) offer hope.

6. EMPLOYMENT TOGETHER

Unemployment is a tragedy which the churches have sought to confront, often together. That work must continue. There must be life after ACE. The time has come for the churches to research the way forward. The government should be asked to fund such exploration of self-help possibilities. Large employers, who have been so helpful to the community, should be asked to second managers to help the churches develop employment schemes.

7. LEISURE TOGETHER

Everyone of goodwill in Northern Ireland wants to see fair employment, which means integrated employment. But I also appreciate the difficulties of achieving it when other aspects of life are segregated. While I recognise the need for more than worship to be shared *within* a single church's parish, so as to build up the sense of a faith-community, I feel the moment is right to question the *amount* of segregated leisure activity sponsored by our individual churches. Several speakers at this conference claimed that the churches supported a form of apartheid in leisure. Is there really any need, eg. for different denominations to have their own badminton clubs, perhaps in a small town where resources at a leisure centre or in a church hall could be usefully shared? We were delighted to hear of youth groups seeking out their counterparts in other denominations. Could this be expanded? Could the older members of our congregations also be provided with the opportunity to relax with, and where there have been divisions perhaps be reconciled to, people from other churches? Finally, the generosity of the people of Birmingham, themselves sadly affected by our troubles, in playing host to the young people of New Mossley on holiday together was praised at the conference. So many people in this part of the world cannot afford a holiday. Our churches should work to provide them (young *and* old) with the opportunity of a break from their routine. Why not work together in seeking to provide the leisure of time away?

I would therefore ask all our churches locally to consider:

(a) whether any of their leisure activities could be shared

and

(b) whether we can work together to find the resources (or the generosity of others) to fund holidays for those who cannot otherwise afford a break.

Moreover,

(c) A call to action must go out to local councils of churches in the other parts of these islands and further afield - on the continent of Europe, in the USA and Canada. Can they work together in offering hospitaity?

8. ORGANISING TOGETHER

The churches must reorganise their structures for co-operation. The CCCCW, for example, could be an even better vehicle if the churches looked again at their contribution to it and their structuring of it. For instance, perhaps the churches could second some of their young clergy to work as development or field officers. The churches must also challenge the secularisation of community relations. The Community Relations Council is a potentially great vehicle for reconciliation but does its Council have any church representatives (not necessarily clerical)? The Cultural Traditions Group has funded two valuable conferences on varieties of Irishness and Britishness, but have they not completely ignored the religious dimension to our lives here? No doubt part of the problem has been the churches' reluctance to work together and to face controversy. That must change.

9. PEACE TOGETHER

Violence must be confronted by the churches being seen to mean what they say at funerals, by isolating the men of violence and by building up structures and relationships of justice through reconciliation. The unity, bravery and generosity in the face of violence, which we have seen in the weeks since the conference are a shining example of Christians together acting for peace.

10.   PRAYER TOGETHER

I would ask all our churches to emulate the SHEPHERD group who pray together at lunchtime on the last Saturday of each month in St Francis' church in the docks area of Belfast.

SHared
Ecumenical
Pray to
Hear the word
Enlighten our minds
Renew our commitment to the
Divine in our lives

So the call to action is a call for:

1. Talking Together
2. Media Together
3. Education Together
4. Families Together
5. Caring Together
6. Employment Together
7. Leisure Together
8. Organising Together
9. Peace Together
10. Prayer Together

APPENDICES

EDITORIAL NOTE:

The CCCCW hope that inter-church community groups will want to discuss together the messages of this book. It occurred to me that some further texts might help us reflect on how the churches can work together for reconciliation. This is personal selection. I would like to thank those who have given their permission to reproduce these documents.

1. GOOD SAMARITAN

Luke 10 v 25-37

'On one occasion a lawyer came forward to put this test question to him: "Master, what must I do to inherit eternal life?" Jesus said, "What is written in the Law? What is your reading of it?" He replied, "Love the Lord your God with all your heart, with all your soul and with all your mind; and your neighbour as yourself." "That is the right answer," said Jesus; "do that and you will live."

But he wanted to vindicate himself, so he said to Jesus, "And who is my neighbour?" Jesus replied, "A man was on his way from Jerusalem down to Jericho and he fell in with robbers, who stripped him, beat him, and went off leaving him half dead. It so happened that a priest was going down by the same road; but when he saw him, he went past on the other side. So too a Levite came to the place, and when he saw him went past on the other side. But a Samaritan who was making the journey came upon him, and when he saw him was moved to pity. He went up and bandaged his wounds, bathing them with oil and wine. Then he lifted him on to his own beast, brought him to an inn, and looked after him there. Next day he produced two silver pieces and gave them to the innkeeper, and said, 'Look after him; and if you spend any more, I will repay you on my way back.'

Which of these three do you think was neighbour to the man who fell into the hands of the robbers?" He answered, "The one who showed him kindness." Jesus said, "Go and do as he did."'

2. EMMAUS

Luke 24 v 13-35

'That same day two of them were on their way to a village called
Emmaus, which lay about seven miles from Jerusalem, and they
were talking together about all these happenings. As they talked
and discussed it with one another, Jesus himself came up and
walked along with them; but something kept them from seeing who
it was. He asked them, "What is it you are debating as you walk?"
They halted, their faces full of gloom, and one, called Cleopas,
answered, "Are you the only person staying in Jerusalem not to
know what has happened there in the last few days?" "What do you
mean?" he said. "All this about Jesus of Nazareth," they replied, "a
prophet powerful in speech and action before God and the whole
people; how our chief priests and rulers handed him over to be
sentenced to death, and crucified him. But we had been hoping that
he was the man to liberate Israel. What is more, this is the third day
since it happened, and now some women of our company have
astonished us: they went early to the tomb, but failed to find his
body, and returned with a story that they had seen a vision of angels
who told them he was alive. So some of our people went to the tomb
and found things just as the women had said; but him they did not
see."

"How dull you are!" he answered. "How slow to believe all that the
prophets said! Was the Messiah not bound to suffer thus before
entering upon this glory?" Then he began with Moses and all the
prophets, and explained to them the passages which referred to
himself in every part of the scriptures.

By this time they had reached the village to which they were
going, and he made as if to continue his journey, but they pressed
him: "Stay with us for evening draws on, and the day is almost over."
So he went in to stay them. And when he had sat down with them at
table, he took bread and said the blessing; he broke the bread, and
offered it to them. Then their eyes were opened, and they recog-

nised him; and he vanished from their sight. They said to one another, "Did we not feel our hearts on fire as he talked with us on the road and explained the scriptures to us?"

Without a moment's delay they set out and returned to Jerusalem. There they found that the Eleven and the rest of the company had assembled, and were saying, "It is true: the Lord has risen; he has appeared to Simon." Then they gave their account of the events of their journey and told how he had been recognised by them at the breaking of the bread.'

3. CONCLUSIONS OF THE INTER-CHURCH REPORT, 'VIOLENCE IN IRELAND'

(a) In spite of the complicated historical and social issues involved and without prejudice to any legitimate political aim, we find unanimously that there is no justification in the present situation in Ireland for the existence of any paramilitary organisations.

(b) It follows that we see no justification for the campaigns of bombing and killing being carried on in Northern Ireland, in the Republic of Ireland and in Britain.

(c) We uphold the right of any group to express its views in peaceful demonstration and in seeking electoral support.

(d) We recommend that the Churches actively support peace and reconciliation movements.

(e) While we recognise that the authorities can make mistakes or be guilty of abuses, we recommend that the Churches jointly remind their members that they have a prima facie moral obligation to support the currently constituted authorities in Ireland against all paramilitary powers and that to do so is not in any way to prejudge longer-term political and constitutional developments. In particular, where an individual has information about violent activities of paramilitary organisations he or she may be assuming a personal moral responsibility if, after taking account of all the personal, family and other dangers involved, he does not put such information before the authorities. Furthermore, the Churches should be prepared to offer strictly confidential advice through their clergy to their members when faced with these terrible questions.

(f)   We recommend that the Churches support the principle of a Bill of Rights to protect minorities. We are in favour of extending the functions of the Commissioner of Complaints in Northern Ireland.

(g)   We suggest the setting up of a Christian Centre of Social Investigation which would conduct research into problems underlying social and communal unrest and would monitor continuously progress made in removing the basic grievances of discrimination and injustice within civil society that are related to the occurrence of violence. Other problems to be investigated underlie our further recommendations and they are problems which must not be shelved if such a centre cannot be established.

(h)   We recommend action by the Churches to ensure that their worship is not exploited by paramilitary organisations at funerals and commemorations.

(i)   We recommend all possible support for the family as a social unit, both through Christian pastoral care and through practical measures set out in the Report.

(j)   We recommend urgent experiment and enterprise in the Youth Service designed to make an appeal to those sections of youth hitherto not attracted to its activities. We urge further effort to establish and maintain interdenominational activities for youth.

(k)   We hold that the Churches should set an example to society in the place they give to women thus encouraging them to take their rightful, confident place in society.

(l)   We call for a sustained and far reaching programme of education within the Churches themselves by which their members may be made more aware of the political and social implications of Christianity for Irish society as well as of the democratic methods available for promoting justice and peace.

(m) We urge upon the attention of the Joint Committee appointed to monitor mixed marriages the special circumstances existing in Northern Ireland.

(n) We recommend the establishment of a Joint Committee to consider closer contact and co-operation between Roman Catholic and other schools.

(o) We regard the growth of community awareness in many areas as potentially one of the more positive developments of recent years and we urge local congregations to make every effort to play a part in these developments.

(p) We suggest that all political leaders should be encouraged to see their task as that of reaching a just agreement with their opponents rather than of achieving victory over them; and that to this end they should be open to any reasonable settlement proposed.

Source

Report of a working party appointed by the Irish Council of Churches and the Roman Catholic Joint Group on Social Questions (1976) pp. 20-3.

4. CULTURAL HERITAGE

RELIGIOUS EDUCATION

Objective 1   Pupils should be able to demonstrate an informed awareness of the shared, diverse and distinctive aspects of their cultural heritage.

By the age of 8 pupils should be able to:
- observe basic details about their family and home and note similarities and differences with those of neighbours and friends, such as, given name/Christian name;
- begin to acquire knowledge of simple customs associated with shared religious festivals, such as Easter, Christmas;
- be aware of shared sacraments, such as baptism and communion;
- begin to know about some shared customs, festivals and stories of patron saints, identifying associated symbols, such as Easter eggs, shamrock, St Brigid's crosses.

By the age of 11 pupils should be able to:
- undertake a comparison of the external and internal physical aspects of the major churches within the locality, recognising the shared Christian heritage;
- know about and begin to understand the shared and diverse features associated with worship, such as altars, communion tables, and also know about and begin to understand practices of worship such as prayer, singing, communion, reading and sermons.

By the age of 14 pupils should be able to:
- understand in greater detail the shared and distinctive aspects of worship, such as prayer, communion and the significance of the Bible;

- deepen their understanding of shared and different forms of worship from more than one traditional belief system.

By the age of 16 pupils should be able to:
- identify and explore questions about moral issues, considering these in the context of the different religious traditions, noting what is shared and what is diverse;
- consider and reflect upon the churches' shared and differing responses to moral issues.

Objective 2   **Pupils should be able to demonstrate a knowledge and understanding of the interaction and interdependence, continuity and change in the cultural process.**

By the age of 8 pupils should be able to:
- observe ways in which members of families provide and care for each other;
- observe some of the ways in which we depend on each other in the home and school;
- record the many ways we care for others in our community.

By the age of 11 pupils should be able to:
- investigate and record how the knowledge of customs, festivals, religious beliefs and practices are passed from generation to generation;
- gain an insight into the significance of the Bible for men and women down the ages;
- know and understand in a variety of ways the interdependence of people in the local community and how and why this interdependence has changed over tine, such as in the contribution of monasteries, churches, schools and hospices;
- know and understand the inter-relatedness of the Christian tradition in the British Isles, such as St Patrick, St Columba and Iona.

By the age of 14 pupils should be able to:
- know and understand the contribution both past and present of the Christian tradition in this island to Europe and the wider world;

– be aware of the ways in which people have suffered both physically and mentally for their beliefs, and have contributed to the suffering of others in times past and present.

By the age of 16 pupils should be able to:
– know about the work of relief agencies such as Oxfam, Trocaire, Tearfund, Christian Aid and begin to analyse their different approaches towards alleviating suffering within the world, and the extent of interaction between a range of relief agencies;
– discuss and critically evaluate the moral issues raised by natural and man-made disasters and the responses of the developed world;
– consider continuity and change in religious life such as the changing roles of women and men in Christian Ministry.

Objective 3   **Pupils should be able to demonstrate an awareness of the international and transnational aspects of today's society.**

By the age of 8 pupils should be able to:
– investigate the transitional origins of customs associated with religious festivals such as Christingle, Christmas trees from Germany, carols from France.

By the age of 11 pupils should be able to:
– begin to know about and understand the origins and meanings of a range of religious and cultural festivals, such as Christmas, May Day;
– know about and understand the transitional origins and influences upon forms of worship in Northern Ireland, such as Latin and the Book of Common Prayer.

By the age of 14 pupils should be able to:
– know about and understand some aspects of the beliefs and traditions of people from outside the British Isles who have brought their religion to Ireland, such as, Huguenots, Moravians and Jews.

By the age of 16 pupils should be able to:
– understand the transitional aspects of the major world religions, such as the way they transcend national boundaries;

– consider the Christian response to the influence of multinational organisations;
– be aware of the customs and influence of groups who have come to Northern Ireland in recent years, such as Chinese and Indian communities.

5. E.M.U.

RELIGIOUS EDUCATION

Objective 1   Interdependence

Pupils should develop a knowledge and appreciation of interdependence within the family, within the local community and within the wider world.

By the age of 8 pupils should:
- know and understand that generally people live together in families and within communities and that as a result people depend on each other in different ways;
- know and understand that people also behave in self-centred ways;
- know and understand the parts played by different people in the religious life of church and school.

By the age of 11 pupils should:
- know and understand that families were arranged in different ways at different times and places; in particular, pupils should know about the Judaeo-Christian basis for families as exemplified in the Old and New Testaments;
- know and understand something of the role of the churches in their community and in the wider world, in caring for people.

By the age of 14 pupils should:
- begin to investigate the extent to which people from different religious traditions within Northern Ireland co-operate in different contexts;
- have further developed their knowledge and understanding of the role of the churches in their community and in the wider world, in caring for people;

– know about and understand aspects of the role of mission
between churches in Ireland, Britain, Europe and the rest of the
world such as the work of Columba and Columbanus and
modern missionary activity both Protestant and Catholic.

By the age of 16 pupils should:
– explore the nature of and be able to assess the consequences of
integration and segregation in Northern Ireland in different
contexts;
– know about, understand and be able to assess the religious and
socio-economic reasons for family patters;
– know about, understand and be able to evaluate alternatives to
family life-styles such as communal living;
– know about and understand the religious dimension to matters
of international concern, such as:
    distribution of world resources
    freedom of conscience and speech
    green issues
    issues of race
    nuclear issues
    gender issues

Objective 2 - Cultural Traditions

Pupils should develop a knowledge and understanding of the
similarities and differences between the cultural traditions which
influence life in Northern Ireland.

By the age of 8 pupils should:
– know that there are similarities and differences in the ways in
which people celebrate the major religious festivals such as
Christmas and Easter;
– be familiar with a range of Bible stories.

By the age of 11 pupils should:
– begin to know about the religious denominations of Northern
Ireland;
– know and understand that places of worship belonging to the
religious denominations in Northern Ireland have similarities
and differences;
– know and understand the interrelationship between worship
and the design of churches.

By the age of 14 pupils should:
- know about and begin to understand the major similarities and differences in the practices of worship of the different denominations in Northern Ireland;
- explore what is meant by the terms Protestant and Catholic - historically and today.

By the age of 16 pupils should:
- know that there are Christian traditions which are not easily classified in Catholic/Protestant terms, such as the Orthodox Churches, the Society of Friends and the Mennonites;
- know about and understand some of the similarities and differences in the worship of the three major monotheistic faiths;
- investigate the nature of Christianity in its various traditions as a worldwide movement.

Objective 3 - Understanding Conflict

Pupils should develop a knowledge and understanding of conflict in a variety of contexts and of approaches to its resolution by non-violent means.

By the age of 11 pupils should:
- be able to identify aspects of conflict within themselves, and between themselves and others;
- read and discuss a range of Biblical material focused on conflict and its resolution;
- appreciate, in a variety of contexts, how conflict can cause personal suffering.

By the age of 14 pupils should:
- have begun to understand the nature of conflict within the individual, the family, the peer group and the school, and should know about a range of strategies for reducing it;
- know and begin to understand something of the historical dimension to religious conflict;
- know and begin to understand that there is a religious dimension to the communal tensions in Northern Ireland;
- know and begin to understand something of the work of individuals, voluntary agencies and churches in reducing tension in Northern Ireland.

By the age of 16 pupils should:
–   know and understand that people affected by conflict can experience differing emotions and reactions and investigate how religious faith can be helpful in alleviating anger, fear and distress;
–   know and understand how the religious dimension to the Northern Ireland conflict is similar to and different from the religious dimension to conflicts in other parts of the world, such as the Arab-Israeli conflict, Apartheid in South Africa and the Moslem/Hindu/Sikh question in India/Pakistan;
–   know and understand the role of the churches and voluntary agencies in seeking to reduce conflict in Northern Ireland and throughout the world;
–   explore issues of religious tolerance, inter-church debate and inter-faith debate.

6. THE CHURCHES CENTRAL COMMITTEE FOR COMMUNITY WORK (CCCCW)

The origins of the Committee lie in the disturbances of the early 1970s. A means had to be found to fund two Advice Centres, one in Derry and one in Belfast. Legislation forbade the funding of particular religious denominations. An Inter-Church body was then created to bye-pass the legislation. But beyond that technical matter, the churches were attempting to do what was in their power to mitigate the bad effects of sectarian strife and massive urban redevelopment. That seems to be still the reason the Committee is necessary.

The Chairman is the Rev Tom Craig. Tom O'Connor is the Development Officer. Wilma Beatty is the Secretary. Each church (Church of Ireland, Methodist, Presbyterian, Roman Catholic) can nominate four people to the Committee. The Central Committee meets quarterly, with an executive committee carrying on work between those meetings. There are sub-committees on the Schools' History Project, Inter-Church Community Action Groups and Training, Youth and Practical Issues. The CCCCW initiates projects, eg. to consider facilities for family support and to reflect on the reasons for emigration among those seeking higher education. The CCCCW can be contacted at:

44 Ballylesson Road
Belfast BT8 8JS

Telephone: (0232) 826409

7. COMMUNITY RELATIONS COUNCIL

The Community Relations Council is an independent organisation, whose purpose is to promote community relations and the recognition of cultural diversity. It is engaged in developing work in the following areas:

1. Supporting the work of existing organisations and encouraging the emergence of new organisations dedicated to promoting mutual understanding, to encouraging cross-community contact and co-operation, and seeking to resolve intercommunity conflict.

2. Working with the full range of public bodies, work and professional groups, community, and voluntary organisations, to assist them in developing the contribution which they can make to improving community relations.

3. Increasing the awareness and appreciation of the existence and validity of the different cultural traditions in Northern Ireland, and exploring how such differences can be handled positively.

The Council is at present engaged in developing the above work through:
–   organising conferences, seminars and workshops which will foster the debate about community relations and cultural diversity.
–   providing information and advice to groups who wish to develop their work to include community relations activities as all or part of their work task.
–   encouraging projects and programmes which will promote knowledge and understanding about differing aspects of cultural heritage in Northern Ireland.
–   training programmes which will increase mutual understanding and which will enable people to develop confidence in

tackling together issues of prejudice, sectarianism, intimidation, and conflict.

– grant aiding groups who wish to develop community relations and cultural traditions activities, or assisting such groups in finding finance from other sources.

(The Council itself at present administers funding schemes which are aimed at assisting Inter-Community activities, Local Cultural Traditions work, Media Projects, and the production of Publications).

The Council is funded by Government, and is managed by a Council who are drawn from the reconciliation, work and community, and cultural sectors of Northern Ireland.

For further information on any of the above areas of activity, please contact the Development Officer with particular responsibilities for reconciliation work, or the Director, at:

6 Murray Street, Belfast BT1 6DN, N.Ireland.

Telephone: (0232) 439953
Fax: (0232) 235208

8. JOHN WESLEY, LETTER TO A ROMAN CATHOLIC

Dublin
18th July 1749

My Dear Friend

1.   You have heard ten thousand stories of us, who are commonly called Protestants, of which, if you believe only one in a thousand, you must think very hardly of us. But this is quite contrary to our Lord's rule, 'Judge not that ye be not judged'; and has many ill consequences, particularly this - it inclines us to think as hardly of you. Hence we are on both sides less willing to help one another, and more ready to hurt each other. Hence brotherly love is utterly destroyed; and each side looking on the other as monsters, gives way to anger, hatred, malice, to every unkind affection, which have frequently broke out in such inhuman barbarities as are scarce named among the heathens.

2.   Now, can nothing be done, even allowing us on both sides to retain our own opinions, for the softening our hearts towards each other, the giving a check to this flood of unkindness, and restoring at least some small degree of love among our neighbours and countrymen? Do not you wish for this? Are you not fully convinced that malice, hatred, revenge, bitterness, whether in us or in you, in our hearts or yours, are an abomination to the Lord? Be our opinions right or be they wrong. They are the broad road that leads to destruction, to the nethermost hell.

3.   I do not suppose all the bitterness is on your side. I know there is too much on our side also. So much, that I fear many Protestants (so called) will be angry at me too for writing to you in this manner, and will say, 'It is showing you too much favour; you deserve no such treatment at our hands'.

4.   But I think you do. I think you deserve the tenderest regard I can show, were it only because the same God has raised you and me from the dust of earth, and has made us both capable of loving and enjoying him to eternity; were it only because the Son of God has bought you and me with his own blood. How much more, if you are a person fearing God (as without question many of you are) and studying to have a conscience void of offence towards God and towards man?

5.   I shall therefore endeavour, as mildly and inoffensively as I can, to remove in some measure the ground of your unkindness, by plainly declaring what our belief and what our practice is; that you may see we are not altogether such monsters as perhaps you imagined us to be.

A true Protestant may express his belief in these or the like words.

6.   As I am assured that there is an infinite and independent Being, and that it is impossible there should be more than one, so I believe that this one God is the Father of all things, especially of angels and men; that He is in a peculiar manner the Father of those whom he regenerates by His Spirit, whom He adopts in His Son as co-heirs with Him, and crowns with an eternal inheritance; but in a still higher sense the Father of His only Son, whom He hath begotten from eternity.

I believe this Father of all, not only to be able to do whatsoever pleaseth Him, but also to have an eternal right of making what and when and how He pleaseth, and of possessing and disposing of all that He has made; and that He of His own goodness created heaven and earth and all that is therein.

7.   I believe that Jesus of Nazareth was the Saviour of the world, the Messiah so long foretold; that being anointed with the Holy Ghost, He was a prophet, revealing to us the whole will of God; that He was priest, who gave Himself a sacrifice for sin, and still makes intercession for transgressors; that He is a king, who has all power in heaven and in earth, and will reign till He has subdued all things to Himself.

I believe He is the proper, natural Son of God, God of God, very God of very God; and that He is the Lord of all, having absolute, supreme, universal dominion over all things; but more peculiarly our Lord, who believe in Him, both by conquest, purchase and voluntary obligation.

I believe that He was made man, joining the human nature with the divine in one person; being conceived by the singular operation of the Holy Ghost, and born of the blessed Virgin Mary, who, as well after as before she brought Him forth, continued a pure and unspotted virgin.

I believe He suffered inexpressible pains both of body and soul, and at last death, even the death of the cross, at the time that Pontius Pilate governed Judaea under the Roman Emperor; that His body was then laid in the grave, and His soul went to the place of separate spirits; that the third day He rose again from the dead; that He ascended into heaven; where He remains in the midst of the throne of God, in the highest power and glory, as mediator till the end of the world, as God to all eternity; that in the end He will come down from heaven to judge every man according to his works, both those who shall be then alive and all who have died before that day.

8. I believe the infinite and eternal Spirit of God, equal with the Father and Son, to be not only perfectly holy Himself, but the immediate cause of all holiness in us; enlightening our understandings, rectifying our wills and affections, renewing our natures, uniting our persons to Christ, assuring us of the adoption of sons, leading in our actions, purifying and sanctifying our souls and bodies, to a full and eternal enjoyment of God.

9. I believe that Christ by His apostles gathered unto Himself a Church, to which He has continually added such as shall be saved; that His catholic (that is, universal) Church, extending to all nations and all ages, is holy in all its members, who have fellowship with God the Father, Son and Holy Ghost; that they have fellowship with the holy angels, who constantly minister to these heirs of salvation; and with all the living members of Christ on earth, as well as all who are departed in his faith and fear.

10. I believe God forgives all the sins of them that truly repent and unfeignedly believe His holy gospel; and that at the last day all men shall rise again, every one with his own body.

I believe that, as the unjust shall after their resurrection be tormented in hell for ever, so the just shall enjoy inconceivable happiness in the presence of God to all eternity.

11.   Now, is there anything wrong in this? Is there any one point which you do not believe as well as we?

But you think we ought to believe more. We will not now enter into the dispute. Only let me ask, if man sincerely believes thus much, and practises accordingly, can any one possible persuade you to think that such a man shall perish everlastingly?

12.   'But does he practise accordingly?' If he does not, we grant all his faith will not save him. And this leads me to show you in few and plain words what the practice of a true Protestant is.

I say, a true Protestant: for I disclaim all common swearers, Sabbath-breakers, drunkards; all whoremongers, liars, cheats, extortioners; in a word, all that live in open sin. These are no Protestants; they are no Christians at all. Give them their own name; they are open heathens. They are the curse of the nation the bane of society, the shame of mankind, the scum of the earth.

13.   A true Protestant believes in God, has a full confidence in His mercy, fears Him with a filial fear and loves Him with all his soul. He worships God in spirit and in truth, in everything gives Him thanks; calls upon Him with his heart as well as his lips at all times and in all places; honours His holy name and His Word, and serves Him truly all the days of his life.

Now, do not you yourself approve of this? Is there any one point you can condemn? Do not you practise as well as approve of it? Can you ever be happy, if you do not? Can you ever expect true peace in this or glory in the world to come, if you do not believe in God through Christ, if you do not thus fear and love God?

My dear friend, consider: I am not persuading you to leave or change your religion, but to follow after that fear and love of God without which all religion is vain. I say not a word to you about your opinions or outward manner of worship. But I say, all worship is an abomination to the Lord, unless you worship him in spirit and in truth, with your heart as well as your lips, with your spirit and with your understanding also. Be your form of worship what it will, but in everything give Him thanks, else it is all but lost labour. Use whatever outward observances you please; but put your whole trust in Him, but honour His holy name and His word, and serve Him truly all the days of your life.

14.   Again, a true Protestant loves his neighbour - that is, every

man, friend or enemy, good or bad - as himself, as he loves his own soul, as Christ loved us. And as Christ laid down His life for us, so is he ready to lay down his life for his brethren. He shows this love by doing to all men in all points as he would they should do unto him. He loves, honours, and obeys his father and mother, and helps them to the uttermost of his power. He honours and obeys the King, and all that are put in authority under him. He cheerfully submits to all his governors, teachers, spiritual pastors and masters. He behaves lowly and reverently to all his betters. He hurts nobody by word or deed. He is true and just in all his dealings. He bears no malice or hatred in his heart. He abstains from all evil-speaking, lying and slandering; neither is guile found in his mouth. Knowing his body to be the temple of the Holy Ghost, he keeps it in sobriety, temperance and chastity. He does not desire other men's goods; but is content with that he hath, labours to get his own living, and to do the whole will of God in that state of life unto which it has pleased God to call him.

15.   Have you anything to reprove in this? Are you not herein even as he? If not (tell the truth), are you not condemned both by God and your own conscience? Can you fall short of any one point hereof without falling short of being a Christian?

Come, my brother and let us reason together. Are you right, if you only love your friend and hate your enemy? Do not even the heathens and publicans so? You are called to love your enemies, to bless them that curse you, and to pray for them that despitefully use you and persecute you. But are you not disobedient to the heavenly calling? Does your tender love to all men - not only the good, but also the evil and unthankful - approve you the child of your Father which is in heaven? Otherwise, whatever you believe and whatever you practise, you are of your father the devil. Are you ready to lay down your life for your brethren? And do you do unto all as you would they should do unto you? If not, do not deceive your own soul: you are but a heathen still. Do you love, honour and obey your father and mother, and help them to the utmost of your power? Do you honour and obey all in authority, all your governors, spiritual pastors and masters? Do you behave lowly and reverently to all your betters? Do you hurt nobody by word or deed? Are you true and just in all your dealings? Do you take care to pay whatever you owe? Do you feel no malice, or envy, or revenge, no hatred or bitterness to any man? If you do, it is plain you are not of God; for all these are the tempers of the devil. Do you speak the truth from your heart to all men, and that in tenderness and love? Are you an Israelite indeed, in whom is no guile? Do you keep your body in sobriety, temperance and chastity, as knowing it is the temple of the Holy Ghost, and that if any man defile the temple of God, him will God destroy?

Have you learned, in every state wherein you are, therewith to be content? Do you labour to get your own living, abhorring idleness as you abhor hell-fire? The devil tempts other men; but an idle man tempts the devil. An idle man's brain is the devil's shop, where he is continually working mischief. Are you not slothful in business? Whatever your hand finds to do, do you it with your might? And do you do all as unto the Lord, as a sacrifice unto God, acceptable in Christ Jesus?

This, and this alone, is the old religion. This is true, primitive Christianity. Oh, when shall it spread over all the earth? When shall it be found both in us and you? Without waiting for others, let each of us by the grace of God, amend one.

16.   Are we not thus far agreed? Let us thank God for this, and receive it as a fresh token of his love. But if God still loveth us, we ought also to love one another. We ought, without this endless jangling about opinions, to provoke one another to love and to good works. Let the points where in we differ stand aside: here are enough wherein we agree, enough to be the ground of every Christian temper and of every Christian action.

O brethren, let us not still fall out by the way. I hope to see you in heaven. And if I practice the religion above described, you dare not say I shall go to hell. You cannot think so. None can persuade you to it. Your own conscience tells you the contrary. Then, if we cannot as yet think alike in all things, at least we may love alike. Herein we cannot possibly do amiss. For of one point none can doubt a moment: God is love; and he that dwelleth in love, dwelleth in God and God in him.

17.   In the name, then, and in the strength of God, let us resolve, first, not to hurt one another; to do nothing unkind or unfriendly to each other, nothing which we would not have done to ourselves. Rather let us endeavour after every instance of a kind, friendly and Christian behaviour towards each other.

Let us resolve, secondly, God being our helper, to speak nothing harsh or unkind of each other. The sure way to avoid this is to say all the good we can, both of and to one another; in all our conversation, either with or concerning each other, to use only the language of love, to speak with all softness and tenderness, with the most endearing expression which is consistent with truth and sincerity.

Let us, thirdly, resolve to harbour no unkind thought, no un-friendly temper towards each other. Let us lay the axe to the root of the tree; let us examine all that rises in our heart, and suffer no disposition there which is contrary to tender affection. Then shall we easily refrain from unkind actions and words, when the very root of bitterness is cut up.

Let us, fourthly, endeavour to help each other on in whatever we are agreed leads to the Kingdom. So far as we can, let us always rejoice to strengthen each other's hands in God. Above all, let us each take heed to himself (since each must give an account of himself to God) that he fall not short of the religion of love, that he be not condemned in that he himself approveth. O let you and I (whatever others do) press on to the prize of our high calling: that, being justified by faith, we may have peace with God through our Lord Jesus Christ; that we may rejoice in God through Jesus Christ, by whom we have received the atonement; that the love of God may be shed abroad in our hearts by the Holy Ghost with is given unto us. Let us count all things but loss for the excellency of the knowledge of Jesus Christ our Lord; being ready for him to suffer the loss of all things, and counting them to dung, that we may win Christ.

I am,
Your affectionate servant, for Christ's sake,
John Wesley.

9. CAHAL DALY

John Wesley's 'Letter to a Roman Catholic' is quite a remarkable document for its time, which was not an age noted for ecumenical charity. It was still a time of polemic and prejudice. In Ireland, religious repression was still in place. Catholic emancipation was still eighty years away. All the more, therefore, do the spirit and tone of this letter evoke our admiration. Indeed, nearly two hundred and fifty years later, the letter can still be read as a moving and relevant contemporary appeal to members of all our churches.

The concluding words of that [first] paragraph are still, to our shame, verified in our daily experience in Northern Ireland. Both Catholic and Protestant communities are challenged by these words, for the word 'Protestants' can be replaced by the word 'Catholics' as circumstances require.

John Wesley goes on to outline the statement of a 'true Protestant's' belief. This could in fact equally stand as a statement of Catholic faith. As John Wesley admits, the Catholic will wish to add more elements of belief, insisting however that these are not extraneous additions to, but rather elements of or deeper implications of spiritual truth. The Catholic, however, is bound to agree with John Wesley's conclusion that: 'Here are enough (points) wherein we agree, enough to be the ground of every Christian temper and of every Christian action'.

John Wesley also outlines 'the practice of the true Protestant', while humbly admitting that some do not live up to the ideal. Once again, the Catholic will find in John Wesley's words an excellent statement of what we know we as Catholics are called to be, while admitting that in practice we fall far short of the ideal. Indeed, Catholics could well take these paragraphs of John Wesley's letter as topics for examination of conscience at a retreat or before confession.

The ecumenical challenge could scarcely be better put in Ireland in our time than in the words of John Wesley's Letter. A programme of ecumenical endeavour for Ireland in our time would still have to include his appeal to both Catholics and Protestants: 'If we cannot as yet think alike … let us always rejoice to strengthen each other's hands in God …'

The letter has been republished in connection with the Catholic-Methodist Conference for 27-30 October 1989 in Belfast. It was an inspired thought to link together the celebration of the 250th anniversary of the Aldersgate conversion of John Wesley and the 200th anniversary of the death of Alphonsus de Liguori, the founder of the Redemptorists. Both these initiatives must make an important contribution to the 'ecumenical conversion' to which all the Churches are being called at this time. I may be permitted to quote some words which I used three years ago at the rededication of St Colmcille's Church in Belfast:

Ecumenical contacts are an imperative duty and an urgent need in our country. They are essential for removal of mutual misunderstandings and prejudices, which foster suspicion and fear. For the love of our land, for the sake of both our communities, above all, for the love of Christ, let us place ecumenism high on our Christian agenda.

The imperative and the urgency grow greater year by year. May the spirit of the two great 'men of devotion, saints for all seasons', who were John Wesley and Alphonsus de Liguori, inspire us in our ecumenical task.

10. RECENT DEVELOPMENTS

(A personal view from Simon Lee)

This book goes to press exactly one month after the conference on which it was based. Thanks to the publishers, particularly Brian Walker, the Deputy Director of the Institute of Irish Studies at Queen's, and the printers, it should appear only a month or so later, in time for Advent. The main hope, of course, in offering this book to the people of Northern Ireland is that its publication will act as a spur to action. But what has happened in the month of October? Is there any sign of a positive response to the call to action, in advance of this book?

The first sign of hope was that those who attended the conference produced many suggestions for developments. In response, the CCCCW is already working on a register or guide to inter-church groups. It is organising local conferences on inter-church work throughout Northern Ireland for 1991. Four specific areas (family, youth, employment and prayer) have been identified for inter-church developments. The executive committee of the CCCCW has to consider plans to expand its own contribution and to find the funds to extend the services it can offer. So the CCCCW has certainly been active, above and beyond inspiring this record of the conference.

A second source of encouragement was the helpful coverage of some of the media, from BBC TV in Northern Ireland, to The Irish Times in Dublin, and The Guardian in England. This in turn led to widespread interest in the CCCCW's work of reconciliation.

But the most important activity, as always, has been the work of those who have given witness to the need for Christians to work together. I do not just mean those who have come together in various parts of Northern Ireland to launch new inter-church groups, much as I am delighted to see them. The CCCCW has been working with these people. But in the midst of a very violent month in Northern Ireland, the bereaved and their churchmen have given us all a lead towards reconciliation.

For example, when Dermot McGuinness and Steven Craig were killed by the UFF and the IRA within minutes of each other in North Belfast on Tuesday 16 October, the two families, Catholic and Protestant, reached out to one another. At the former's funeral, the Catholic Bishop Anthony Farquhar said: 'Your families have also been united in giving to all of us an outstanding example of dignity in the face of suffering, gentleness in the face of violence, resurrection in the face of crucifixion'. At the latter's funeral, the Church of Ireland Bishop Gordon McMullan said that the responsibility for overcoming the men of violence lay with the law but also with 'the moral strength of people working together towards better understanding and mutual respect'.

Another example of great Christian charity in the face of violence came with the murder of RUC dog handler, Sam Todd, shot by the IRA in Belfast city centre on the morning of Saturday 13 October. Not only did it emerge that Sam Todd had been a Good Samaritan in the Comber area where he lived with his wife and sons, he was a Good Samaritan in death. He had signed a donor card and he was kept alive until recipients were ready to receive various organs in transplant operations.

On Wednesday 24 October, the IRA killed several people in separate incidents involving 'human bombs'. The people of the Derry border area, Catholic and Protestant, came together to pay their respects and to assert their wish to live together in peace. On the following Saturday two of the victims were buried. Both were Catholics, one Patsy Gillespie had been forced to drive a bomb in Derry, the other was a young soldier, Cyril Smith, a Royal Irish Ranger, who had died trying to deal with another human bomb at Newry. The latter died as a Good Samaritan. As Father Anthony Doran said at his funeral, 'Cyril Smith, who could have run to safety, gave his life by running back into danger for his friends'. The Catholic Bishop of Derry, Edward Daly, denounced the IRA in the clearest of terms, at the funeral of Patsy Gillespie:

'I believe that the work of the IRA is the work of the Devil. I say that very deliberately and I say it as a Catholic Bishop charged with preaching the gospel.'

'Jesus Christ said: "By their fruits ye shall know them"'.

'The fruits of the IRA are strewn all over Europe, from a murdered infant in West Germany, to murdered tourists in Holland, to murdered pensioners in Enniskillen, to murdered Good Samaritans in our own city'.

The next day, the Church of Ireland Archbishop, Robin Eames, endorsed the words of Bishop Edward Daly and emphasised that this condemnation applied to all those perpetrating violence, on all sides.

A few days earlier, Archbishop Eames had told his diocesan synod in Armagh that 'there are now more Protestants and more Roman Catholics in Northern Ireland than ever, who desire the path to peace'. He saw 'more co-operation between Roman Catholics and Protestants in community affairs than I can recall in my lifetime'.

So the month of October has seen great sadness but the churches, the people, of Northern Ireland will not be deflected from working together for reconciliation.